ACCEPT THIS C

Also published by SPCK:

Kenneth Stevenson and Michael Perham
Waiting for the Risen Christ (1986)

edited by Kenneth Stevenson
Liturgy Reshaped (1982)

ACCEPT
THIS OFFERING

The Eucharist as Sacrifice Today

Kenneth Stevenson

SPCK

First published in Great Britain 1989
SPCK
Holy Trinity Church
Marylebone Road
London NW1 4DU

British Library Cataloguing in Publication Data

Stevenson, Kenneth W. (Kenneth William),
    1949–
    Accept his offering : the eucharist as
    sacrifice today.
    1. Christian church. Eucharist
    I. Title
    264'.36

    ISBN 0–281–04405–8

Typeset by Photoprint, Torquay, Devon
Printed in Great Britain by
Bocardo Press Ltd, Didcot

CONTENTS

✤

PREFACE

❖

This little book stems from a long acquaintance with the many ways in which Christians of different lands and different ages have approached the Eucharist and given it a sacrificial colouring.

It is a fascinating story. For me it really began when as a teenager I spent many a summer holiday in various European countries savouring a rich diversity at Holy Communion. I can remember the excitement of an elaborate offertory procession on a Sunday morning with the Taizé community, where everything that the community was trying to be and do was somehow caught up in that ritual act. I can remember the gaunt and dignified environment of a Danish Lutheran cathedral, as the pastor poured from a huge silver flagon, organ music wafted from the west gallery like incense. I can remember a Polish Catholic priest elevating high the freshly consecrated host as a gesture of showing the bread to the people and at the same time presenting it to God. I can remember a bearded Greek village priest pausing at the iconostasis, half way through the liturgy, and telling us who to pray for before he went in to the holy of holies.

All that was soon given the kind of analytical critique that a conventional theological education could offer, and I found myself as a student probing into the background of these texts and contexts, increasingly amazed at the variety of ritual action, liturgical text, and – perhaps most import-ant of all – the attitude of the ordinary pious worshipper.

In due course, I was able to write up my analysis during a sabbatical semester at the University of Notre Dame, Indiana. The resulting publication, *Eucharist and Offering* (published in 1986 by Pueblo, New York), tries to tell the historical story of the Eucharist in all its variety and also to

vii

point to some areas where there could be some healing, rather than controversy. I am grateful to Bishop Mark Santer, Anglican Co-Chairman of the second Anglican-Roman Catholic International Commission (ARCIC II), who saw the ecumenical potential of that work and contributed its foreword. In the following pages, I present my ideas for a wider audience (readers wanting fuller documentation must have recourse to that larger book). I am also grateful to Michael Perham and Bryan Spinks for their comments and suggestions.

My basic thesis is this. Sacrifice, so far from being an outdated way of understanding the Eucharist, lies at the very heart of what we are doing at the Lord's Table. More than that, the variations of faith and practice that we see all around us in contemporary Christianity are signs of hope and life. They also indicate that we *need* the view of communion-sacrifice for good liturgies, healthy pieties – and a better world.

At the end of the day, this tricky but crucial facet of the Supper of the Lord is about the praying life of the Church, and it is therefore appropriate that I dedicate this little book to my own praying community, the people of Holy Trinity and St Mary's, Guildford, whom I have served as Rector since August 1986. Their warmth and vigour are a source of constant thankfulness.

Kenneth Stevenson
Pentecost 1988

1

SPIRITUAL SACRIFICES?

✣

. . . and like living stones be yourselves built into a spiritual house, to be a holy priesthood, to offer spiritual sacrifices acceptable to God through Jesus Christ.

(I Peter 2:5)

1

Sacrifice is the theme of this book and throughout the pages which follow we shall try to show that the idea of sacrifice at the Lord's Supper is no mere appendage to the eucharistic repertoire but is as central as those which have gained a steady place in popular parlance, like the very idea of meal-fellowship.

But as soon as 'sacrifice' is mentioned in Christian discourse, hands are thrown up, embarrassment settles in, and attempts are made to get rid of the word altogether. Roughly speaking, five objections are raised in order to create or maintain this language-barrier.

First, there is the basic psychological reaction many people have to the mere mention of the word. It can conjure up feelings of revulsion and fear, because it can depict wilful destruction, the needless end of life, and the shedding of blood. To put it bluntly, many people think sacrifice belongs to the history books – to the study of 'outdated', 'pagan' religions. They may well back up their case by suggesting that when it is applied to the Eucharist a quaint picture comes to mind of a medieval priest standing with his back to the congregation, muttering weird Latin prayers at a side altar, and 'offering the sacrifice of the Mass' to no apparent avail. Contemporary ways of celebrating the Eucharist 'in the round' and the introduction of the vernacular liturgy in the Roman Catholic Church have done a lot to dispel these fears. The number of simple communion tables that have recently appeared in Roman Catholic Churches would have delighted many of the Reformation Fathers, with their emphasis on the meal aspect of the Eucharist. But that makes the question all the more acute. What is the point of still using the term 'sacrifice' today?

The thrust of this book is to argue that the sacrifice is a powerful *metaphor* which conveys something of the power, the passion, the feeling of the Eucharist that seems to have gone out of some of our more staid, clinical celebrations. Today's world needs that metaphor. This will not turn us into cannibals, or simple-minded medieval peasants. We are not sacrificing Christ in a crude manner on a stone slab, nor are we offering the Mass with a 'special intention', nagging God in order to get something out of him. Rather, we are meeting around that altar table to celebrate the power and passion of our God as we are able to perceive and feel his presence. In a world that knows about suffering in its own way, the metaphor of sacrifice has returned, with a new and vibrant meaning, for our own generation.

Secondly, we are sometimes told that the idea of sacrifice at the Eucharist is not found in the Bible. This objection is the most fundamental of all, and it is the one most likely to come from the very Protestant side of Christianity, which protests that Christ died once and for all and there is nothing that Christians can do at the Supper other than commemorate that unique and drastic event. To them, much of the language used by Catholics, especially terms like 'offering mass', is contrary to Scripture and the result of accretions that entered the Latin Tradition at a time when the Church was insufficiently alert.

It is true that the New Testament nowhere speaks of the celebration of the Holy Communion as a sacrifice in the way of priests offering animals and cereal-offerings in the Old. Christ's death has swept all that away. But the metaphor of sacrifice is strong throughout the New Testament. The Last Supper is charged with an atmosphere of sacrifice, as Jesus goes onward to his death, and as the disciples share with him in their last meal together. Impending death and mutual solidarity make the Eucharist *cost*. For this reason the metaphor of sacrifice reappears, for example in the quotation from 1 Peter cited at the beginning of this chapter, which speaks of the people of God offering *spiritual* sacrifices. Here the author is trying to apply the image of the Jewish temple, now destroyed, to the new community.[1] Sacrifices that are spiritual are no less real, rather the reverse. The spiritual house, which is the Church, is the house in which the Spirit of God is at work, the sphere in which the Spirit is operative. Like the author of this book, the writer is trying to *widen* notions of sacrifice that have been too narrow, too specific. It is hard to imagine the term 'spiritual sacrifices' not including acts of worship, especially the Eucharist itself.

A third objection that is frequently raised is that sacrifice is an outmoded term, a barbaric notion for which our sophisticated modern world has no room. To borrow a tired epithet of iconoclasm, the word is 'irrelevant'. It is true that animal sacrifices abounded in the ancient world. Indeed, it was the failure of many early Christians to offer sacrifice to the emperor that brought the new religion into disrepute and created the phenomenon of martyrdom whereby Christians could 'witness' to the Lord by dying for their faith in him. One early Christian martyr, Cyprian of Carthage, probably knew of the practice of *human* sacrifice among the Baal-worshippers of his part of North Africa, which had long been colonized by Phoenicians, whose religion the people of Israel had to learn to shun in Old Testament times.

But for all that, the aroma of sacrifice persists. At one level, modern literature[2] keeps throwing up figures that can only be described by 'sacrifice' motifs, the most salient example of which is in William Golding's novel, *Lord of the Flies*. And the very term 'holocaust', which was once used to refer to burnt-offerings in the Jewish Temple has since World War II gained a horrific place in the dictionary of human violence. Whenever we meet to break bread in remembrance of Christ, our actions and the lifestyle we are trying all the time to make our own are necessarily sacrificial.[3]

A fourth objection that is sometimes made centres round the renewal of eucharistic worship that has figured so prominently in our generation. The Churches have grown together so much, and we are now celebrating the Eucharist so much more with ever-increasing numbers of communicants, that it seems a pity to introduce what almost seems like a dirty word into the atmosphere, as it will only bring strife and disagreement. Catholics and Protestants fought over the word in the sixteenth century – and they have since. But now that we are learning to speak of the Eucharist as a 'dynamic memorial' of Christ's death (a term acceptable to many on both sides of the traditional divide), does not the reintroduction of a difficult concept threaten to spoil our newly-found concord?

That is a superficial view. Not for one moment do we lament the tremendous advances in eucharistic faith and practice over the past century. The mainstream Churches of the West have rediscovered the Eucharist. But a price has been paid for it. Michael Ramsey's wry observation of the ever-repeated Old Testament sacrifices could equally well be applied to our current preoccupation with celebrating the Holy Communion on every conceivable occasion: 'For all its ceremonial elaboration, the system could not conceal hints of an inner scepticism about its own validity.'[4] We need to recover the *cost* of the Eucharist in liturgy and piety for a generation that has learnt to 'have a Eucharist' in much the way that it likes to drop in for a cup of tea. If we do not do that, we risk running down a cul-de-sac. In my view, to understand the Eucharist as a sacrifice is one way of achieving such a necessary balance.

The answer lies in releasing from the Eucharist its own inner potential to judge the people around it, and that includes the people who come to celebrate it as well as the society that immediately abuts it. It *costs* to take those words seriously. It *costs* to stand at that Table under the shadow of Calvary, in the faith of Easter morning, in the hope of the Kingdom dawning and bringing about the new age. It *costs* to turn what is often the mere verbalization of yet another liturgical text into the powerful context of God's redeeming love, where healing takes place between people, where the elderly feel valued rather than rejected, and where the middle-aged unemployed have a self-esteem that goes beyond sitting in a nice pew and taking the collection.

A fifth objection is perhaps the most esoteric but it is still crucial to the discussion because it is where some liturgical chickens come home to roost. We shall be arguing for a much wider view of sacrifice than has been customary in the Christian West. Nonetheless, there are two particular points in most eucharistic rites where the contrary views of sacrifice become peculiarly sensitive.

The first is at the point when the bread and wine are placed on the table (or else simply uncovered). What is said by way of interpretation can speak volumes. The president may say nothing at all. The president may quote I Chronicles 29 ('Yours, Lord . . .). The president may yet use words from the Roman Missal, 'Blessed are you . . . through your goodness we have this bread to offer . . .' Other formulations decidedly more upmarket sacrificially may also be used at this point. Hymnody can also supply an important backdrop.

The second point is in the eucharistic prayer. Immediately after the recital of the words of institution, there follows a prayer of remembrance (called the anamnesis) which in effect states why the Eucharist is being celebrated, what it intends to be and to do. Some rites (e.g the 1975 British Methodist) speak only of making the memorial with the bread and cup; others (e.g ASB, Rite A, EP 3) cautiously refer to the bread and cup as things which 'we bring before you'; others again (e.g. Roman, EP II and EP III) are happy to 'offer' the bread and cup in memory of Christ's death. As we shall see later on, the permutations behind these texts are almost numberless. They have been debated carefully in recent years and they are therefore important areas of convention within the discipline of having a eucharistic rite at all.

The fifth objection states that these two areas are where sacrifice is sensitive – and that they should be left well alone. Protestants can refuse to say anything when the elements are placed on the table, while Catholics can say elaborate things. (It is interesting to note that both these options are built into the Alternative Service Book.) But that objection is once again a superficial one. Liturgy is often about rich ambiguity – about words and actions that can mean different things, according to the context of the people who are worshipping. But there are really two sorts of ambiguity. One is the kind of ambiguity that results when issues are fudged. Another sort is the offspring of the subtle experience of paradox, which holds together two opposite viewpoints *both* of which are necessary for the whole truth to reach out in its full force. My own conviction is that for liturgical text and piety the bread and wine are neither ritually offered nor withheld from God's power. That very subtle idea needs exploring. But first, we need to turn to the way in which texts are produced for Christians today.

2

New service-books have recently appeared all over the Western world, varying from the Roman Missal (1970), through the British Methodist Service Book (1975), to the Church of England Alternative Service Book (1980). In each case, scholars, executives, and prayer-writers were charged with the task of producing new services that would reflect the drift of liturgical renewal as it has swept through the Churches this century. Now, some years on, is the time for stock-taking, particularly as in all these Christian communities neo-conservative noises have been heard crying out for a return to 'the good old days'. In my own parish we live with this tension quite happily. The larger of the two churches uses the Alternative Service Book 'Rite A' for the main service, a Sung Eucharist at 10.00 a.m., whereas the smaller (and older) of the churches has, more by accident than design, become one of the few places in the area where the Book of Common Prayer is used for virtually all the services. It is good for the old and the new to coexist.

When the new books are compared with their respective predecessors, the differences that emerge are seen to be as much to do with culture as with doctrine. The three modern service books I have mentioned have as much in common with each other as they have with their antecedents. Thus, for the Eucharist, the new Missal, the Methodist rite and the ASB adopt almost exactly the same shape, the main difference being that the confession comes at the start of the Roman rite, whereas it can come either at the beginning or before the offertory in ASB. On the other hand, the language of the 1570 (so-called 'Tridentine') Missal, which had been the result of centuries of evolution in liturgical Latin, is now replaced by a different style of Latin, but this is infrequently heard, as the new rites are usually celebrated in the various vernaculars of the Roman Catholic world. A similar observation can be made about the ASB: Cranmer's English is replaced by a different type of language, which is hardly as resonant, though many people find it satisfying, in spite of the continued attempts by the cultural establishment to bring the Prayer Book rites back in, with a higher profile.

There are many complex issues here. Liturgical revision, today as in previous centuries, is the art of the possible; there is always a tension at the time of liturgical ferment between those who want to conserve and those who want to innovate. Similarly, the way in which new rites express many of the insights already existing (or recently intro- duced) in pastoral practice is a good measure of their success, or at least of their commendability. But it is undeniable that a new kind of liturgical language has had to be brought to birth (with some undue haste), one might almost say prematurely, and the child so born arrives as the product of an unpoetic and somewhat jarring environment.

Nevertheless, the way in which these liturgies handle

sacrifice is a case-study of the way in which scholarship and politics meet – and clash. When the new Roman rite appeared in draft form in 1965 (the so-called 'Missa normativa'), the offertory rites were drastically simplified, so that the priest said very little at the preparation of the gifts of bread and wine, quite unlike the somewhat fulsome provisions of the 1570 Missal. However, the final text in 1970 redressed this balance, and also inserted two Jewish-inspired prayers ('Blessed are you, Lord God of creation') which were intended to be recited at a said Mass but only whispered at a sung celebration (because of an offertory chant). These prayers became so popular that they are almost invariably used, and their use has spread to other Churches as well. The other main change in 1970 (which was followed by other Churches too) was the introduction of alternative eucharistic prayers, which would recount the tale of salvation-history in a variety of forms, and stress the role of the action of the Holy Spirit, virtually for the first time in the life of the Roman rite. When it came to the way sacrifice was to be handled in all these rites, we find Roman Catholics, Anglicans, Methodists, and Presbyterians all took considerable care in reappraising their traditional positions, both at the presentation of the gifts (the offertory) and in the eucharistic prayer. For Roman Catholics, the new rite was a drastic departure, for their old eucharistic prayer (now EP I) was laden with the language of offering. The 1662 Prayer Book, however, was reticent about the offertory; at the consecration it spoke of the death of Christ 'once and for all', but after Communion described the Eucharist as 'this our sacrifice of praise and thanksgiving'. The new rites have loosened things up. We shall return to them in more detail later. Meanwhile, it is important to note two critical questions posed by the writing of new texts.

First of all, because of the inherently ambiguous character of good liturgical prayer, it has to bear repetition, it has to resound, it should not attempt to define, it needs to match many different kinds of experience (or at least not confront them negatively). This means that there should be an element of the *paradoxical* about images in prayer, especially when used in relation to important theological areas, such as what the Eucharist is setting out to *do*.

The passage quoted from 1 Peter includes an effective rhetorical device for pointing up the paradoxical nature of the Christian community. We are 'a spiritual house', we offer 'spiritual sacrifices' (1 Peter 2:5) . . . and the passage goes on in similar vein. Strangely, one of the criticisms levelled against the ASB is that it veers to the side of biblicism, yet it does not seem to learn the lessons of biblical paradox at its most central points, such as when describing how the Eucharist is a sacrifice. Rather than using this sort of device, the compilers had recourse to using the bald language of definition:

> We remember his offering of himself, made once for all upon the cross.

Criticism of the same kind can be made of the new Roman prayers, particularly in EP IV, where the bald language of definition goes well beyond tradition:

> We offer you his body and blood.

It is a pity that a new prayer, written in the thick of the ecumenical movement, should make the Reformation appear to have been fought for nothing. In no way does the Church offer Christ's body and blood to the Father, for that kind of bluntly realistic language destroys the subtlety of sacrifice as a *metaphor*.

The second question about liturgical language reinforces the importance of ambiguity and paradox. In two recent studies, Leslie Houlden[5] has suggested a model for the way in which the language of doctrine developed in the New Testament. He notes four stages:

Stage 1 may be called *impact*. This is the impact of Jesus on the believer, the immediacy of the Christ-event, touching lives in all sorts of ways.

Stage 2 may be called *experience*. This happens when groups are corporately aware of the impact having taken place, and of the fact that nothing will ever be the same again.

Stage 3 may be called *expression*. This is when the experience of the impact has to be put into some means of communication, both for those outside (evangelism) and for those inside (worship and teaching).

Stage 4 may be called *formulation*. This is the crucial stage when the expression of the experience of the impact has to be agreed upon by diverse groups, so that they may come to a common mind in a way that can make sense to a wider community, including posterity.

Houlden maintains that at each stage, edges are blunted, and this is most noticeable between Stage 3 (expression) and Stage 4 (formulation). The same (I would suggest) can operate in worship, so that the basic individual experience is ignored or even denied by the formulation used in a random liturgy. But there is a significant difference. Unlike doctrine, liturgy cannot evolve from the one to the other without some degree of ambiguity, because liturgy is its own language, and it needs both clarity and resonance – in other words what might be called 'creative ambiguity'. Contrariwise, liturgies which are written with the express purpose of defining suffer from two deficiencies. They have evolved too rapidly, without real gestation. They narrow down meanings and contexts so that they lose their own freedom (different kinds of usage) and the freedom of the worshipper (different ways of relating to the language used).

Because of the rush to produce new liturgies, and the fact that many of the compilers perhaps knew too much selective tradition for their own good, none of the eucharistic rites mentioned so far has been entirely successful in expressing Eucharist and sacrifice in a coherent manner that tackles the real doctrinal issue, and says that the sacrifice of Calvary is once and for all, but that the Eucharist is performed as a recalling of that offering, in union with Christ's prayers for us at the Father's right hand. Simply by putting that into words for the reader to assimilate is difficult enough. But it becomes considerably easier when we have the humility to recognize it not as a neat, packaged piece of doctrine, but as a paradox, a union of opposites, almost a self-contradiction. We need to produce prayers that do just that. We need *time* to write them.

3

In many places where the Eucharist is celebrated frequently, the question is sometimes asked, What goes before it? or, How do people prepare for it? Pastoral practice comes readily to mind, informed by various Christian traditions.

Scene 1. A celebration of the Byzantine liturgy. I am standing next to a friend, and it is the first time I attend this particular service with any knowledge of its development. (Liturgists sometimes do go to church with the severe handicap of knowing too much about what is going on). After fifteen minutes or so, the priest appears from the north door of the large iconostasis, carrying a book. He processes round and re-enters the sanctuary area through the central door. I whisper to the next person to me (who does want to know what is going on!), 'That's when the liturgy *used* to begin, with the Little Entrance of the Book of Gospels – the priest has just placed it on the altar. If a deacon were here, he would have carried out that task.'

The first few minutes, before the Little Entrance, had been taken up with the Office of the Three Antiphons, which used to be separate from the Eucharist. However, by a process of assimilation it has come to be an inseparable part of the Liturgy, expanding on the preparatory rites, which are already lengthy and elaborate.

Scene 2. A celebration of the Danish Lutheran liturgy. People arrive by 10 a.m., when the threefold 'Kyrie' bells are rung, and the priest appears in vestments at the altar. An organ voluntary then plays, probably chosen to reflect the season of the year, or possibly based on one of the hymns to be sung in the service. A 'choir-deacon' (in lay dress) leads an introductory prayer, asking for God's grace in the hour of worship that is to follow. Then, and only then, comes the first hymn, a substantial offering of praise, preceded and followed by short improvisation. The time is perhaps 10.15 when the Collect for the day is intoned from the altar.

Scene 3. A weekday Eucharist in a French Benedictine community. The community has already gathered, informally and without fuss. The Office of Terce is chanted, consisting mainly of psalmody, but ending with a short reading and prayers. Silence follows. Two monks (a priest and a deacon) appear at the lectern for the Mass. The atmosphere is contemplative and entirely in accord with the tradition of the Order and the architecture of the building.

Scene 4. An Anglican Parish Communion. The noise level up to (and after) the last moment is intense. Wardens and sidespeople rush around to distribute leaflets, service booklets and hymn books. Families pour in, many of whom have endured that delightful experience, Sunday family breakfast, with eventemperedness, especially from the adolescents. The rector somehow blows the whistle on all of this (the organ voluntary has barely been audible) and proceeds to introduce the service with a lengthy series of notices. Such notices may be replaced by a 'warm-up' of choruses, informal singing, or music of some other kind.

All these four traditions give witness to the fact that down the ages people have felt the need to stand back a bit from the Eucharist before celebrating it. Those pre-communion services still popular in the Highlands of Scotland are another example. Each is entirely in accord with its setting and performs the same function: Byzantine repetition, Lutheran music, monastic psalmody, Anglican activity (and Scots Presbyterian penitence). What each does is express the need for a liturgical infrastructure into which the Eucharist fits. But it goes deeper than that. Such developments are about a basic attitude to the Eucharist that is by its very nature contradictory, even paradoxical. We want to approach that Table, yet we want also to hold back. We feel the need to assert our right to stand before God and offer spiritual sacrifices, yet we are aware of our unworthiness to do so. The official rites give little help here in their modern forms, except perhaps in their introductory material. Some churches start the Sunday Eucharist in an ancillary building, and get the notices and other preparatory material out of the way before the whole body, and not just those who are wearing colourful vestments, processes into church. Whatever is done, the liturgical psychology of this continuing need for an infrastructure is appealing, curious, inconsistent, and profoundly Christian.

From each of these scenes there is a sacrificial nuance that can enrich us. In the Byzantine rite, it is clear that *all* worship is sacrifice, and such language is used at strategic points in the liturgy to show this important fact, so that we have no confining of offering to a particular moment. In the Lutheran rite, hymnody plays a significant role in the *déroulement* of the liturgy, so much so that there is almost something sacred even about singing. It is therefore right that the preparatory prayer *precedes* the first hymn; the lips that offer praise must first pray. In the monastic tradition, psalmody is the backbone of spirituality, and the way the Eucharist is placed in context is by the offering of psalms to the living God. Finally, that Anglican noise, however fraught, at least admits the effort that getting families to church on time entails, but also expresses that worship is a social activity, and the community's business must be got out of the way before the eucharistic sacrifice is celebrated.

But the infra-structure should not just inform us of the need for a 'wider' view of the sacrifice of Eucharist, and the awesome character of beginning the celebration. It should also challenge us to take more seriously what we said earlier about making the right connections between worship and what goes on outside the church building once the service is over. We can only learn to trust worship if it becomes so much part of us that we can take the rough with the smooth;

that we can take the spiritual jolts that a good homily or an unusual hymn will give us; that we can enjoy God's presence among us, in whatever form that may take, according to our very different circumstances.

Meanwhile, the liturgies that we use do not stand still. Unlike the Bible, they do not have canonical status, and it is right that they should change, preferably more than once every four hundred years. But movements in liturgy are subject to the same shifts in the pendulum that other areas of human creativity know well. A period of great activity is likely to be followed by one of reaction, even conservation. This is probably going to be the case with the new rites that have been produced over recent decades. But if what we have said so far is true, then we can hope for four developments in the future.

First, we can expect minor adjustments in the texts that we have, and perhaps the production of supplementary material that will make up for some of the inadequacies of what we use at present. For our present theme, such texts should be more adventurous, and more sensitive to the need for paradox in expressing the inexpressible quality of Christian truth, not least in how it is both a sacrifice and how it is not a sacrifice.

Secondly, we can do much to improve the pastoral practice of the Eucharist, particularly in the build-up to the celebration, so that the almost archetypal need for preparation is adequately fed, not just with reverence and godly fear, but with time and human space to approach the unapproachable.

Thirdly, we need to reappropriate the piety of sacrifice at the popular level, so that it is seen as it was of old, a collective offering by the whole people, rather than something done by the priest for the congregation.

Fourthly, we need to lose our fear of the language of sacrifice, and see it not just as a useful adjunct to the eucharistic vocabulary, but as a central way of understanding the nature of the God we worship.

NOTES

1. See E. G. Selwyn, *The First Epistle of St. Peter* (London, Macmillan, 1946), pp.165ff., and pp.282–98. I am also indebted to Professor Barnabas Lindars, SSF, for this discussion.
2. See F. Young, *The Origins of the Christian Doctrine of Sacrifice* (London, Darton, Longman & Todd, 1978), and F. Young, *Sacrifice and the Death of Christ* (London, SPCK, 1975). See also, for a more general discussion, Godfrey Ashby, *Sacrifice: its Nature and Purpose* (London, SCM, 1988).
3. Robin Green, *Only Connect: Worship and Liturgy from the Perspective of Pastoral Care*. London, Darton, Longman & Todd, 1987.
4. Michael Ramsey, *Jesus and the Living Past* (Oxford, Clarendon Press, 1980), p.65.
5. Leslie Houlden, 'Trying to be a New Testament theologian', in A. E. Harvey, *Alternative Approaches to New Testament Study* (London, SPCK, 1985), pp.134ff. See also a fuller discussion in J. L. Houlden, *Connections: The Integration of Theology and Faith* (London, SCM, 1986), pp.61ff.

2

ATTENTION!

✤

. . .that with meek heart and due reverence, they may hear and receive thy holy word, truly serving thee in holiness and righteousness all the days of their life.

(Book of Common Prayer)

1

When these words were first written, they appeared in the course of a lengthy block of prayer in the 1549 Communion Office corresponding to the eucharistic prayer of old. This particular section was part of the intercession, in the course of which prayers and supplications are made for different needs, religious and secular. The quotation forms part of the petition for the congregation, right in the heart of this prayer.

In 1552, however, the whole prayer was moved to a new position, just after the presentation of the alms, and that is the place in the English Prayer Book where it has stayed ever since. What, it might be asked, is the point of this prayer here?

Whatever position it occupies, it underlines one of the principal insights of the sixteenth-century Reformers when it came to liturgy. They wanted, quite simply, to make a stronger link between Word and Sacrament. In their eyes, for far too long (though not for quite as many centuries as some of them thought) liturgical practice, if not the liturgical texts of the Latin Church also, had severed the connection between reading and preaching of the Word on the one hand, and administering and receiving the sacrament on the other.

A new direction, clearly, had to be found. In 1549 Cranmer makes this point with a subtlety and an eloquence not quite so apparent in 1552. For in the 1549 rite, the 'Word' is invoked, with the Holy Spirit, on the gifts of bread and wine, prior to the recital of the Words of Institution. Earlier on, the congregation is to 'hear and receive' this 'Word'. In 1552, however, this connection is lost, for the consecration prayer loses its invocation of Word and Spirit, and the prayer of intercession is moved to an earlier part of the eucharistic liturgy.

Nonetheless, Cranmer's intentions are still laid bare, and the echo of the Benedictus ('that we . . . might serve him without fear all the days of our life, in such holiness and righteousness as are acceptable before him')[1] only serves to emphasize them. The people of God are gathered together for worship, which means, *par excellence*, the hearing and the receiving of God's Word in its widest sense. Cranmer, like the other Reformers, was determined to bring into the domain of public worship the religious psychology of a widened doctrine of God's Word, more faithful to Scripture, more biblically based in its application, and, as his words make plain, more closely connecting the world of liturgy and the world outside to which the worshippers will in due course return. As we saw in the previous chapter, the purpose of worship is to serve God better. So Cranmer's focus on the Word (in 1552, this is the only time that this term is used in the entire Eucharist) is deliberately vague, not because he wants to be imprecise, but rather because he sees the point of a rich ambiguity when it comes to liturgical language.

Critics of the Reformers have been quick to assert that their understanding of sacramental worship was paltry, and that they did not have enough knowledge of worship in antiquity to live up fully to their pretensions that they were, indeed, compiling truly scriptural liturgies based on the practice of the primitive Church. But do liturgical revisers ever manage such a task? Every age of liturgical activity has to respond to what it has received in its own way. For all that our generation knows much more about the evolution of the eucharistic prayer (and, we hope, has shown this, too), it is easy to imagine a future generation writing a history of the twentieth century's liturgical reform, in which we appear to be very much children of our age, wrapped up in our own concerns, and even projecting some of them on to our ancient, and less ancient, liturgical models.

In the sixteenth century, there was obviously a need to 'widen' the Word. The Bible was slowly becoming available to an increasing number of people as a book that would be both accessible and familiar to them. Liturgical books of the Middle Ages included Epistle- and Gospel-Books, and later on these came to be superseded by the Missal, a compact way of producing in one volume all that was necessary for the celebration of the Eucharist. In the Prayer Book tradition, all these books were to be replaced by a Book of Common Prayer, and each church was to have its own Bible. It is hard for us to imagine the change that this would have made on the average congregation of the sixteenth century, whether it was a rural flock, or a city gathering of wealthy burghers, or even an intelligent College community. This is not to say that there were not difficulties. The rural flock might be in Cornwall, made up of the folk who rebelled against the First English Book in 1549, because they could not understand it; their dialect was too rich. Equally, the city congregation could have included religious exiles from Europe who were not anglophone. And the College might easily have numbered in their ranks academics who took a more extreme position over liturgical reform and for whom Cranmer was an outdated conservative.

Such reactions, of course, are familiar in our day. Liturgical reform moves forward organically rather than piecemeal. People are people, and they must be allowed to respond to change in their own way. Nonetheless, such an emphasis on the Word was both significant and lasting. And I suggest that it was both the basic intentions of the compilers of the Prayer Book and the effect that the new rite had on congregations that inculcated what is potentially a timely interpretation of worship as sacrifice. If we look more closely at the liturgy of the word, whether in its

Prayer Book form or in the shape that it now has in most of the modern liturgies, an internal logic becomes apparent. The worshipper begins with some sort of preparatory rite, either as part of the beginning of the liturgy, or as personal, private devotions. Such preparatory material may vary from an introit hymn to the decalogue, but its purpose is to engage the attention of the worshipper in a preliminary way. As all sermon-writers know well, the start of the discourse is the most important of all. That maxim holds good of liturgy as a whole. Then there is a shift away from generalities like the Collect for purity to specifics, like those variable liturgical units that comprise the Collect and lections for the occasion. The Collect's function is to focus briefly on the day's prayer; it is not just intercessory. And the way in which the readings take effect is often, nowadays, bedded down by suitable chants or hymns between them, so that the congregation does not suffer from indigestion at the experience of large chunks of unfamiliar Scripture. Such chants can, of course, serve the very opposite purpose, in that they can take over and provide positive distractions from the purpose in hand. But the hymn before the Gospel, in particular, is a rare occasion to reflect on the readings and sometimes provides a unique opportunity of picking out some aspect of the day's lections and meditating on them.

In the Prayer Book rite, the Creed intervenes between Gospel and Sermon, and it is not entirely clear whether the English Reformers intended the Sermon to be an exegesis of the Gospel-text, though they clearly wanted the Sermon to be Scripture-based, as the Book of Homilies shows. But here, again, we have the progression from particular (Gospel) to general (Creed), and back again to particular (Sermon). In today's liturgies, the Creed usually comes straight after the Sermon or Homily, and there is increasing criticism for this position, since many preachers have an urge that is not without precedent in church history to take the congregation through exegesis and teaching to devotion and prayer. This would make the prayer of intercession a more fitting conclusion to the sermon, but (as we shall see in the next chapter), the intercession has its own inherent balance of general and particular.

How is this scheme sacrificial? It is sacrificial in the sense that the Word of God is offered to the people, for them to 'hear and receive'. (Note the wholesome psychology of the doublet, 'hear and receive', which suggests more than mere cerebral absorption, and points to a deep and profound appropriation of God's Word.) The sacrifice here indicated is not one that is limited by the traditional and rather mannered dialectic of 'manward' and 'Godward'. Here, the sacrifice is God's offering of himself in his Word, and ours in the response of hearing and receiving, and of living lives of holiness and righteousness. The symbolism of sacrifice has been embedded in the Word for centuries by the practice that is being revived in the West of bearing aloft the Book of Gospels at the Introit. More homely but no less direct is that custom, well known in the Presbyterian Church of Scotland, of the beadle carrying in the Bible and placing it on the pulpit at the start of the service. As we shall see, there are many ambiguities surrounding the metaphor of sacrifice. But in carrying the *book* in a significant manner, we are (whether we like it or not) entering a world of symbolism, and with it the world of sacrifice. Here, the Word is being 'offered' to *us*, not in its entirety, but in manageable chunks. To the effect of those chunks we must now turn.

2

Since the Second Vatican Council, the revolution in the Roman Catholic Church has forced many whose loyalties are to a Church of the Reformation to ask themselves what they are being Protestant about. This is not least true of attitudes to the Bible, and not just in liturgy. The Missal of 1970 is accompanied by a Lectionary that is the result of painstaking care on the part of biblical scholars. Instead of the time-honoured Latin Lectionary of Epistles and Gospels, dating mostly from the Middle Ages, we now have an elaborate three-year scheme, with generous provision for Old Testament readings as well as Epistles and Gospels, and even specially selected responsorial Psalmody between the first two lections. Roman Catholics are now more familiar with the Bible than they ever were before. The liturgy becomes harder work for them – and rightly so.

Before we discuss the question of lectionary principles, it is worth reflecting for a space on the nature and purpose of story in the Christian faith. 'Story' has become a popular term recently, for a number of reasons. For a start, it is less technical and obtrusive than 'myth', which poses too many problems even for the best-read person. (For ninety-nine per cent of the population, the word 'myth' means something that isn't true.) There has also been a rise of interest in popular culture, which has had a great effect on the way history is taught in schools and colleges. Even Latin, when it does appear on the curriculum, does not just mean how to address a table; it also involves understanding the how and the why of Roman culture and society. Even in inner urban Manchester, the inhabitants of an area like Hulme become informed of their 'story', which is about the old Victorian housing destroyed during the War and replaced by the present large, impersonal deck-access tenements.

'Story' has had an effect on the way we handle theology. The Christian story is an ambiguous affair, because it is made up of both the general and the particular. It is about the way that God has spoken to whole communities in the past and it is also about the way he speaks to particular communities and individuals now. Each Christian community has its own story, which comes to a head when any change is under discussion. In Methodism every year there is a Church Anniversary, which is often far more real than the Dedication Festival so often celebrated in a routine manner by Anglicans. At the Anniversary, the story is localized and incarnated in a very particular way.

But story is not mere folklore, for if it is it becomes warped and sentimentalized. The Christian story has to be selective, because people and communities cannot take in the whole of salvation-history in one fell swoop. This holds true particularly of the Bible, where in a whole lifetime, or less, there will be particular portions and styles that meet different sets of life experiences. Perhaps one of the reasons for the popularity of story in Christian discourse today is that it safeguards the relationship between individual and community, between unity and diversity. And no preacher with any sense can be unfamiliar with the important developments in biblical exegesis that surround the unity and diversity of the New Testament in general and the Gospels in particular.

But there is another facet to story that sets our reflections on the Word in the liturgy in an even wider context. Story is a way of seeing another nuance in the way a community celebrates its Christian faith. It is binding on the community because it serves to make the community what it is, with its own style, character, concerns, and (when it comes to preaching and intercession) its own tragedies and achievements.[2] And this is what makes 'story' a strong sacrificial metaphor, because of the way it builds up commitment and differentiates who is in the community and who is not. A consequence of this may be that some who are anxious not to sharpen this division any further may be deterred, for boundaries of church membership are a source of increasing tension, not least over such questions as baptism policy.

The Christian story, therefore, is a costly business, because its rehearsal is potentially a transformation of the ordinary into the eternal. Such is the message of the incarnation, and it is bound up with the basic need to read the story of our redemption through the Scriptures, to pray and reflect upon it, and to hear it preached again and again. Perhaps we need to look at this anew in the light of the deeply symbolic context of sacred reading into which we enter every time we celebrate the Lord's Supper. For that takes us into a world whose difference from our own is highlighted by the very fact that the Gospel may well be read from an elaborately-bound volume, between two large candlesticks, whereas the hearers are part of a cosmos of paperback books, multiple-printed, and where the photo-copier is an indispensable tool in parish life and beyond.

Some would say that to juxtapose these two worlds is an artificial arcane exercise. But the very fact of juxtaposition serves to highlight the nature of the story, that it is both general and particular, that it is both special and ordinary, that it is both something that we can hear rehearsed as well as something that we shall never fully understand. Story and parable are close, because Jesus never *defined* his Kingdom, he spoke of it obliquely, he only told his hearers what it might be like. Once again, we encounter the sacrificial character of the story, for its meaning is not always obvious, and it is up to us to try to apply it. The very ritual pattern of rehearsing the story implies that we shall want to return and rehearse it anew, in the possibly quite different context of next week's triumph or tragedy.

This means that lectionaries are important – but they are not of lasting significance. One of the fruits of the liturgical movement has been that those Churches of a more definite Reformed persuasion who never had lectionaries, nor indeed a liturgical year or calendar, are now seeing that they enable congregations to have a varied diet of Scripture, instead of listening to the preacher's tired old favourites. In the Alternative Service Book, the lectionary is based on a two-year scheme put forward in 1967 by the British Joint Liturgical Group, comprising several of the mainstream Protestant Churches of this country. The two-year scheme was originally put together as a selection of the most important passages from the Old Testament, Epistles, and Gospels that could be found. The compilers resist the accusation that it is 'thematic', but that is how the majority of preachers, and many of the laity, perceive it. There is many a Sunday parish newsletter that prints the Sunday Theme in bold letters; and the theme often intrudes into introductions, welcomes, intercessions, and sometimes even the eucharistic prayer. The inherent danger of such a scheme is that it runs the risk of making the liturgy too neat and tidy, and of ironing out the anomalies, ambiguities, indeed that element of 'roughage', that should be a staple part of the Christian diet. While the Roman Catholic Lectionary is not a perfect one, significantly it has been adapted and adopted by many other Churches in North America, South Africa, and Australia. These include Anglicans, Lutherans, Methodists, Presbyterians – hardly Churches that would rush into a new scheme of scripture reading at public worship without pause for careful thought.[3]

Whatever lectionary is used, the same sacrificial criteria apply. The Christian story is still made available and accessible to the people of God. But its riches are more eloquently and systematically handled in the three-year Roman Catholic format, because the Gospels are read in turn and in sequence, so that each evangelist is given a full hearing, and the preacher and community have the chance to enter together into the mind of the gospel-writer over a long space of time. This lectionary, unlike the 1967 Joint Liturgical Group production, has been written for today's people without surrendering to their culture entirely.

3

The Liturgy of the Word has been described as the 'sacrifice of attention'.[4] Here, the offering that is made is not just the fruit of lips that praise, but hearts that are receptive. But in order to be receptive, certain issues have to be got out of the way.

The first is about participation. In the Western Churches today, there has been a spate of participation at many levels of liturgical life. Whereas before, the liturgy was performed largely by the priest at the altar or preaching minister at the pulpit, now there are many different people doing many different things, such as reading lessons, leading intercessions, performing different musical items, and assisting with the distribution of Communion. The Roman Catholic Church appears to have led the way, though it is sometimes hard to tell the difference between one Church and another.

Without for one moment wanting to call a halt to this

exciting phenomenon, it is worth pondering just what participation should mean.[5] It is more than just the particularly gifted who like to show off doing noticeable public deeds that involve a certain dramatic flair. It is more than just getting someone to read or do something who does not want to do it, but has been pressurized because it is somehow needful. It is more than the amount of noise and liturgical fuss that high-level participation necessarily brings in its wake.

Many people, not just those on the fringe of church life, can actually be put off by liturgies that are so aggressively participatory that those who are not so advanced in the spiritual life or so exhibitionist in their personal make-up feel excluded and choked off. It is a well-known fact of sociology that maximum participation does not necessarily bring maximum drawing in of other people; there might even be some exclusion of them. The phenomenon is familiar enough, and abuse of a good development is no argument against the principle.

In practical terms, it probably means having fewer people taking a regular part in these various ministries, so that there is an element of continuity. This cannot, however, be any more than a rule of thumb, because there are some places where the liturgy is necessarily so informal and therefore so sophisticated that wide participation is *de rigueur* – but these are clearly exceptional. In theological terms, it means seeing participation in the liturgy in a wider and a deeper sense than many people realize. Participation in liturgy does not require saying everything that can be said, singing everything that can be sung, and doing everything that can be done. To put it at its bluntest, we need to relearn in our own way for our own generation what it means to *pray* the liturgy, each in his or her own style. For this, worship must be a sacrificial activity, not least when someone is reading the Old Testament lesson with a particularly difficult meaning and context. We also need to relearn what it means to pray the Bible and reflect upon it. In this connection, the renewed emphasis on silence in liturgy is something that is more often than not misunderstood. To be silent corporately is to wait upon God and to listen to him. It means 'Speak, Lord, for thy servant heareth' rather than 'Listen, Lord, for thy servant speaketh'. Once again, to 'hear and receive' God's Word requires being ready to absorb it.

The second problem area concerns meaning. In today's consumer age, one of the pieces of baggage that is usually brought to church is the mind trained by the media to reduce complex truths into instant slogans. Many preachers give in to this, hence the array of slogan-bearing banners and mottoes that adorn many a nave and sanctuary. There is a lot of good in making the Christian faith memorable and there is a strong argument to suggest that much of the material in the Gospels was handed down by the expedient of learning by rote. But slogans and subject-headings can only help along part of the road. The Christian faith is not an easy business and it cannot be reduced into slick titles just because many people today want the meaning of everything to leap to their minds instantly. Newscasters usually begin their programmes by short summaries, delivered in a more stilted tone of voice, with gaps between each summary; they then go through each subject in more detail, in a more animated fashion. The headlines are often helpful and they have to be worked at harder than the main bulletins subsequently delivered because of that. The technique is an object-lesson in the communication of a type of 'news' that is not likely to change in quite the same way.

And yet in many cases, bible readings are introduced in such a way that the 'headline' has very little to do with the 'bulletin', because it consists of an ill-prepared sermonette that imposes a particular meaning on a highly symbolic portion of Scripture. Clearly, this is one of the problems posed by having a lectionary that gives us more choice over two, or three, years than we had before. A lection only read once every two or three years is less likely to be familiar to a congregation than one which comes round every year at the same time. To impose a meaning on Scripture is to take risks, and that means opening the floodgates to the theological predisposition of the person concerned. (I once heard a student introducing a New Testament passage with a desperate attempt to milk from it the medieval notion of the penal substitutionary doctrine of atonement.)

Meaning can be more subtle still, and here the sacrificial flavour can add a helpful dimension to the liturgical diet. The fourth century was the time when many of the classical liturgies underwent their most formative change. In the East (as we shall see in later chapters) it produced some very nuanced ways of describing the work of Christ and the meaning of the Eucharist. Among the great preachers of that era was John Chrysostom, who at Antioch towards the end of that century once described the activity of preaching as a sacrifice. The word he used was not one of the more general words connected with offering and presenting gifts, such as are to be found in the liturgy that bears his name. He used the full-blooded word *thusia*, which is seldom employed in eucharistic liturgy to describe the Eucharist itself. John was nicknamed 'Chrysostom' ('golden-mouthed') because his preaching was so famous, so that for him to describe that function for which he was renowned in so strong a term cannot be coincidental. Was he referring to the agony-and-ecstasy of what it means to stand regularly in the pulpit before the same group of people? Was he describing the process of compiling a fresh sermon on a familiar text? Was he alluding to the experience of having to preach on a difficult subject, but feeling compelled to do so? Was he taking a side glance at the whole liturgy of which preaching is a necessary part?

He was probably including all of this ministry in the word; and that was perhaps why it sprang to mind. Preaching is a sacrifice because it is one of the greatest privileges of ministry in the Church. Whatever tradition is involved, no particular branch of Christendom 'owns' the pulpit, certainly not today. Preaching is a sacrifice because, more than the reading of Scripture (or even the introducing of Scripture into public reading in the assembly), preaching means speaking the good news of the gospel despite knowing that you are going to get it wrong; because the way the preacher applies the gospel to the community is not going to meet everyone's needs, although the preacher must still try.

Many people indulge in so-called alternative ways of preaching, and some of them (like drama and dialogue-sermons) can be effective. But they are no substitute for the real business of one person wrestling aloud with the gospel and proclaiming it aloud. Just as the second part of the Eucharist reaches two high points in the eucharistic prayer (or anaphora) and in the distribution of Communion, so the liturgy of the Word reaches its two high points in the reading of the Gospel and the sermon. The parallel is complete in that gospel text and anaphora are set forms that belong to the community, whereas the sermon and the individual acts of communion are going to be different for each of those concerned.

But most of all, preaching is a sacrifice because it is a means of trying to communicate something about God for his world, and that involves the necessary ambiguity and paradox that are part of the life of God himself. Those who do not take the Word seriously and regard it as a mere prelude to the eucharistic banquet need to heed the solemn periods of the Prayer Book, and thereby 'hear *and* receive' the Word, God's meaning for us.

Finally, there is the question of worship and education. These are frequently confused because many people in practice identify the two. Thematic lectionaries do not help, especially when everything in a service has to fit together so that the theme dictates what the liturgy has to say, and the Word of God seems tamed to the particular fad of the planning group. But while worship and education overlap, they are yet distinct. As Aidan Kavanagh has recently put it:

> Being, like the feast, an end in itself, the liturgy inevitably forms its participants but does not educate them in the modern, didactic, sense of the word. Other media and contexts are available for education. Conflating liturgy and education produces poor education and dissimulated

liturgy. The liturgy, like the feast, exists not to educate but to seduce people into participating in common activity of the highest order, where one is freed to learn things that cannot be taught.[6]

This means lots of things. It means continuing to 'play it slant', and treating public worship as being in parabolic form, where meaning is not necessarily obvious, and where people are enabled to grow in understanding and in the affective aspects of their personality. Many educationalists see in liturgy subtleties of image and symbol they would dearly like to use in their own trade. Those who plan public worship must therefore hold back from predetermining what a liturgy is going to mean and say, and let the liturgy have its own independent life, in which the president and other ministers are the servants, rather than the compères or (worst of all) the dominant figures in control of everything all the time.

Nowhere is this more true than in the sacrifice of attention, the liturgy of the Word, where teaching can only be part of the homily (if that), and where the readings from Scripture need to reflect the diverse character of the Christian faith, and even include a good story or two, to balance other types of sacred lection. Liturgy is something that cannot be taught, because it is part of the activity of the sacrificial God whom we worship, the God whose nature and purpose are not always obvious, though they are always filled with the paradox of a Word that is made flesh, while still remaining infinitely mysterious. In words taken from the Byzantine liturgy before each reading at the Eucharist, 'Let us *attend*'.

NOTES

1. For the development of this prayer, and its sources, see F. E. Brightman, *The English Rite*, Vol.ii (London, Rivingtons, 1925), pp.663ff. and 688ff.
2. For an outworking of these ideas, see W. H. Vanstone, *Love's Endeavour, Love's Expense* (London, Darton, Longman & Todd, 1977).

3. See Michael Vasey, *Reading the Bible at the Eucharist*, Grove Worship Series 94 (Bramcote, Grove, 1986).
4. See Mark Santer, *The Church's Sacrifice* (Fairacres Publications 47, 1975), pp.3ff.
5. See Evelyn Underhill, *Worship* (London, Nisbet, 1936; reprint, New York, Crossroads, 1984), pp.83ff.
6. Aidan Kavanagh, *Elements of Rite: A Handbook to Liturgical Style* (New York, 1982), p.28.

3

PRAYING FOR . . .

⁂

We offer you also this reasonable service for . . .
(Liturgy of St John Chrysostom)[1]

1

The intercession is now so firmly part of the Sunday
Eucharist that it is almost inconceivable to celebrate Holy
Communion without it. Further, the new liturgies have
persuaded us that the proper place to pray for the Church
and the world is towards the end of Liturgy of the Word.
There is an internal logic about it, too, for the Christian is
more likely to be in a position to pray for various needs
when God has been approached at the start of worship, and
the Word has been read and preached.

But to place the intercessions at the end of the Liturgy of
the Word (or the 'synaxis', meaning 'bringing together', as
it is often called) is by no means the only position that it
occupies in worldwide Christianity. The quotation from the
Liturgy of St John Chrysostom is taken from the eucharistic
prayer, which, like nearly all the anaphoras of the Eastern
Churches ends in intercession. Why?

The reason is partly to do with the type of language of
these prayers, partly to do with their length, and partly to
do with their sequence of ideas.

The language of these archaic prayers is rich and varied
and they abound in biblical and patristic images, and they
usually attempt to cover the whole of salvation history. This
means that they are longer (many of them) than the new
eucharistic prayers in use throughout the Christian West
today. But the main theological reason for including
intercession is their shape. With few exceptions, the
anaphoras of the Eastern Churches – for all their prolix

character – have a simple logic about them. They open with a thanksgiving-series for creation, which moves into some kind of catalogue of Old Testament material. They then move forward to the incarnation and praise God for the life and ministry of Jesus. The Last Supper fits into a chronology with the Institution Narrative. Then the prayer takes up the theme of remembrance with the paragraph usually called the 'anamnesis', making the memorial of Christ's death and resurrection, at which point the gifts of bread and wine are often (though not always) offered to God. At this juncture, the prayers change gear by moving from thanksgiving to petition, from 'anamnesis' ('remembering') to 'epiclesis' ('calling upon'). In the epiclesis, the Holy Spirit is invoked upon the gifts of bread and wine and upon the congregation who are going to receive them. Unlike so many Western prayers, which split the epiclesis, so that the gifts are consecrated before the Institution Narrative and the congregation's sanctification is prayed for after it, the Eastern prayers nearly all keep this notion of consecration together in one single petition, 'upon us and upon these gifts'. There are some modern eucharistic prayers, notably those of the Scottish Episcopal, American Episcopal, and Canadian Anglican Churches, which resolutely adhere to this shape.

It is the change of gear from thanksgiving at length to petition that provides the reason for placing intercessions after the epiclesis of these prayers. And the logic is plain; if you are going to pray for the blessing of the Spirit on the Eucharist of the Church, then you might as well pray for the many other concerns of the Christian community that are within its purview. To intercede as a consequence of epiclesis is to hold a theology of the Eucharist that refuses to see it as in any way separate from the 'world'.

Intercession in this particular position probably dates from the late third and early fourth century. It takes several forms, though conventionally they include the Church universal, secular leaders, the suffering, those who travel, crop-sowing and other themes as regular features of these anaphoras. What is interesting is that there are three main linguistic conventions for the start of each separate petition. Either it is 'we pray for', or it is 'remember, Lord', or it is 'we offer . . . for'. The first requires little explanation. The second does not set out to tell God what he does not already know, but rather is based on the assumption that God should 'remember' his people, bearing them in his mind and heart. There is a gesture of pleading that may well accompany the psychology of this type of intercession. The Roman Catholic eucharistic prayers use 'remember', albeit sparingly, at this point too.

But 'we offer for' in intercession requires some explanation, particularly as it raises some Protestant sensitivities that are wary of any view of the Eucharist that is in some way mechanical, manipulating God, using the Lord's Supper as a means towards gaining some aim or purpose.

To 'offer for' is to offer the whole Eucharist, pleading the sacrifice of Christ, in union with his prayers for us at the Father's right hand. There is no sense of presumption, rather the mood of this type of petition is one of dependence upon God. In John Chrysostom's liturgy, the words 'we offer this reasonable service for', occur at three strategic points; first at the start of the epiclesis, second at the start of the intercessions for the living, and third, at the start of the commemoration of the departed. Because the underlying motive is that of pleading, it is important to note that in this tradition intercession is understood to be truly sacrificial, because it is part of the Church's life of witness and service. The 'reasonable service' is the whole Eucharist, not any part of it, and so the best way to inculcate such a 'holistic' view of the banquet to which Christ invites us is to focus those words, 'reasonable service', on the three dimensions that make the Church what it is, namely in the consecration of the gifts and congregation, the strengthening of the whole Church's mission in the world, and the deepening of its awareness of being in communion with those who have gone before us in the faith.

For far too long, Protestants have avoided sacrifice in

intercession, even though the test of sincere intercession is the commitment to do something about what is being prayed for.[2] There is something of self-obligation about such an approach to intercession, and it only becomes suspect when the sacrificial style takes over the entire celebration of the Eucharist, and the Eucharist is celebrated repeatedly for very specific concerns, as was the case in the later Middle Ages. But that pastoral context is no longer with us. The danger today is rather the celebration of the Eucharist in small and narrow pastoral contexts, like select groups; that is why the intercessions are such an important part of the celebration, because they can prevent the ambience of the occasion degenerating into the kind of introspection which frequently characterizes contemporary Christianity. It would be a fine thing if when fresh eucharistic prayers are written for many of the Western Churches the new compositions included intercession as a natural and logical outcome of the epiclesis, when we pray for the blessing of the Spirit on our witness. It would be even finer if the intercessions, wherever they are placed in the service, used sacrificial terms such as 'we offer this reasonable service for . . .'

We have dwelt at length upon the misunderstood and neglected area of intercession in the eucharistic prayer. Its rediscovery could solve two further pastoral problems. One is the tendency to omit the intercession altogether when some special liturgical act, even a baptism, takes place after the sermon. Such an omission is to be deplored. Another reason is that short, varied petitions after the epiclesis could serve to bring a universal dimension to the intercessions, when those which were offered earlier in the service might have tended to be particular in their scope and style. It has been pointed out that the Eastern prayers are fulsome and all-inclusive. Their underlying themes recur in antiquity, and they form the basis of the best of the older traditions. Nowadays, we have become so used to the sequence of Church, secular rulers, community, suffering, departed, that many congregations feel bereft if just one section is passed over. In the Prayer Book of 1549, the secular rulers came before the church leaders, an inversion of the traditional order that neatly expressed Reformation sentiments. Happily, the new Anglican books have returned to the older sequence of subjects, an eloquent way of expressing the supremacy of God over Caesar. But we are in danger of fossilizing this sequence, and of overlooking many of the concerns of the wider community, such as education (in all its forms), research (at all levels), and the saints, because of the drift of priorities that make many well-intentioned intercessors want to pray for their own narrow little world. History is full of lessons here, as witness the fact that for centuries the Roman Catholic Church prayed on Good Friday in its 'solemn prayers' for catechumens that never existed, simply because the text could not be altered.

2

So much for the position of intercessions. What about their rationale?[3] This is even more important, particularly when the impression outsiders receive of many of the intercessions offered in our churches is that God sits above the skies, being nagged by the Church, a community of people determined on self-preservation, which is a purpose they are more likely to achieve through repeatedly asking the deity for the same things, week after week. It is easy to caricature the Christian community. Nonetheless, it would not be untrue to say that intercession is theologically the weakest element in regular worship; hence the oft-quoted burlesque, 'Let us pray – here is the news'.

Long ago, Augustine wrote that 'God does not ask us to tell him about our needs in order to learn about them, but in order that we may be made capable of receiving his gifts.'[4] He was writing at a time when the intercession was still an integral part of the Latin rite of his area. As we shall see, the meaning of intercession is at every stage replete with the sacrificial aspects of the Christian life. It is, essentially, about relationships. First of all, intercession is about our relationship with God. The Christian spiritual tradition, manifested in the Bible and reinforced in the lives of the saints, is one which affirms that God is our friend and companion. It therefore follows that, just as you do not go up to a stranger and ask for £100, you will not begin your relationship with God by demanding what you want at the time. That does not rule out the fact that people arrive in church with *needs*. But it is a strong argument for the tradition that intercessions should not normally *begin* the liturgy. We come to understand the ways of God better if we come to intercession after adoration, after listening to the Word read and preached, and in penitence and faith.

The liturgy is not, however, an isolated event; it is subject to repetition, so that the group of people who pray for a particular person or cause are going to return to pray once more for that person or cause. In the meantime, anything may have happened. For example, the person with cancer may be the subject of a long-term cure that cannot fully be understood. (These occurrences are known, and although they do not prove anything, the fact that they are accompanied by a Christian ministry of healing indicates how they are, at least in part, accomplished.) On the other hand, that person may have been granted a short-term remission, in the course of which the family pull together in a way unknown before, the time being measured no longer in length but in depth. Yet again, that person may have gone to a hastened rest, dying in faith and trust, and without bitterness.

In all these ways, God's gifts can be perceived, and his nature and purpose, if not always understood, at least accepted. Not all intercessions are as tender and sensitive as the topic just mentioned, but a serious and tragic illness highlights the issues. To pray to God is to speak to him, and to listen to him. Very often, it is done in fear and trembling. As Antony Bloom has aptly put it: 'We believe and we do not believe at the same time, and faith shows its measure by overcoming its own doubts.'[5]

Second, the relationship is with those *with* whom we

pray. There is much emphasis today on the corporate, and the Christian community seems to live a somewhat schizophrenic existence, yo-yo-ing from one extreme (the individual) to another (the congregation). The recent reintroduction of the gesture of the Peace has served to underline this important feature of the faith.[6] Once again, a new idea can be trivialized, and many people find it hard to greet the same people Sunday by Sunday precisely because they always sit in the same place. In some congregations, people only greet their in-group, and ignore the stranger. There can be strangers who would find such a greeting a way of becoming part of the flock, and others again who are put off a particular religious club for life.

Once again, however, the sacrificial flavour brings a suggestion of seriousness to the arena of worship. To greet with the Peace is to make a bold assertion about love and equality, and it challenges those who greet one another to live up to those claims when the liturgy is over and Christian witness has to start. Moreover, to pray in company with others, and to be aware of their gifts and foibles, is to make oneself open to the prayerful support that they can bring, a necessary feature that can be discerned as much in the silence that usefully punctuates intercession as in the words that sometimes pour out ceaselessly.

The third level is the relationship with those people *for* whom we pray. And it is those *people*, not those *situations*! A peculiar habit of contemporary society is to dehumanize people, until they become situations, whether on-going, crisis-ridden, or processed. Further, many intercessors think that one should only pray for problems. Bernard Levin's book *Enthusiasms* is subtitled 'An irresistible celebration of the joys of life',[7] a sober reminder that it is often from the so-called secular tradition that the most profound religious truths for a particular generation are cried aloud. But whether the petition is about a problem or about a great achievement (and there should be room for *both*), the underlying message is that you cannot pray *for* someone without in some sense committing yourself to doing something about it. If the concern is local, then that self-sacrifice may mean donations of cash and time and concern. If the concern is on the other side of the world, then that self-sacrifice may mean no more than being well-informed about it, and causing other people who would otherwise be in ignorance to know more about it. The effect of the regular discipline of such corporate intercession is to build up commitment, and make us more Christlike, to put it at its simplest. Praying for other people at a time when they may know that you are praying for them is an experience that millions share on Remembrance Sunday and during the Three Hours on Good Friday. Folk religion suggests that such prayer is more effective for the sheer impact it makes on its own than many care to recognize.

But there are difficulties that are bound to occur in any extended reflection on the meaning of intercession, and they will affect the liturgical assembly as much as, if not in the same way as, the intercessions of individuals or small groups at home. One is *unanswered prayer*. Intercessions which repeatedly mention people by name, and their physical, mental, or spiritual condition, run the risk of demanding from God what he may not give. We mentioned earlier the case of the person with cancer, clearly a serious event. All too often, the way intercessions are put together may imply to the congregation that all it has to do is 'pray hard' (whatever that means) and all will be well. But, however distraught the family and friends must be, to pray for the same particular end, week by week, is to fall into one of the obvious traps of setting God the agenda, rather than praying in a manner that enables us to receive his gifts. This is not to suggest fatalism. But it is to caution Christians to realize that there is a faith that accepts and a faith that rebels and that they belong together. In the rebelling that is part of the personal adjustment to tragedy, it may well be that there are occasions when the local congregation has to express its protest to God, but these should be few and far between, unless they grip a congregation totally. The 'suffering righteous' is a personality deep in the collective memory of the Judaeo-Christian tradition, and the somewhat bland and anaemic periods of Sunday intercessions do not match happily with reality when an event of really serious proportions affects a congregation. Once again, prayer and self-sacrifice walk hand in hand.

Another difficulty could be described as the experience of *the absence of God*. This is an area of basic religious experience which is frequently ignored. Indeed, there are whole sections of the church which are so intent on being joyful that those who, for circumstantial or biochemical reasons, feel that God is absent are made to regard themselves as distinctly second-rate Christians. It is important that such experiences, familiar to experts in the spiritual life, should be recognized, particularly as the absence of God implies that there is a relationship, that there is a person or being from whom one is absent. Clearly, this is more often than not a feature of individual prayer, and yet it can be the experience of a Christian congregation, working through a crisis in its own collective discipleship, towards a new, and perhaps quite different, calling in the wider community. How all of this is 'carried' in intercession is bound to vary, but it should be recognized for what it is – a wilderness experience, a difficult time of aridity, when worship seems lifeless, the sacraments do not mean anything, God appears not to care.

A third difficulty is the theological issue of *prayer and the departed*. Like eucharistic sacrifice itself, it became an emotive issue at the Reformation, because of the medieval piety associated with purgatory, and the repeated Masses for the dead that were offered in order to gain forgiveness of sins for the departed.

Fortunately, there is now a healthier balance. Roman Catholics celebrate thoroughly paschal funerals, which emphasize the Christian hope, and the fact that only God is the judge. Most of the Churches of the Reformation realize that they overreacted in the sixteenth century, and their paltry funeral rites were too abrupt, liturgically inadequate, and pastorally insensitive. It is no coincidence that one of the earliest examples of prayer in relation to the departed comes from the anaphora (eucharistic prayer) of Basil of Caesarea, which is also the first eucharistic prayer to include a full intercession. His text antedates the Reformation controversy. It couches the language and aspirations in terms that are eschatological and biblical, and looks forward to the consummation of all things at the end of time. Reminiscent of the Jewish Passover embolism (an insertion into one of the main prayers, for Jerusalem), it runs as follows:

> Since, Master, it is a command of your only-begotten
> Son that we should share in the commemoration of your
> saints, vouchsafe to remember, Lord, also those of our
> fathers who have been well-pleasing to you from eternity
> . . . [Then follows a list of faithful ones.]
> Give them rest in your presence; preserve us who live
> here in your faith, guide us to your Kingdom, and grant
> us your peace at all times; through Jesus Christ and the
> Holy Spirit.[8]

The sequence of ideas is admirable. The Church celebrates the Eucharist in communion with all the saints and God is asked to remember all of them, to grant them rest in his presence, as the Church on earth awaits the fullness of the Kingdom of God at the last day. Here, perhaps, is a model that may serve usefully to ritualize the reality of Church and saints on the one hand, and Church and departed on the other. If God is the judge, then there can be nothing wrong in offering our solemn prayers in two overlapping *contexts*, the Church and the glory of the saints, and the Church in mourning for particular people, known and still loved.

3

When it comes to putting prayers of intercession into words, history provides many admirable models and some salient lessons. The intercession is one of those parts of the liturgy which has been opened up in recent years. Like other features of the liturgical renewal, the sixteenth-century divide over authority and freedom in the liturgy seems to have given way to a constructive consensus, which may be characterized by the term 'freedom within a framework'. But it can also know its heights and depths, from the flights of beauty of a gifted intercessor who knows the limitations of personality and time, and can somehow make words fit together with good rhythm, to the excruciating and earnest political activist (whether of Right or Left) who will not leave God (or the congregation) alone, with the result that the liturgy loses all its subtlety and power.

There are, at root, four basic styles of intercession. Each has its own disciplines, and they need to be recognized for what they are. The first (and probably the earliest) is the *litany*. It is by nature simple, evocative, rhythmical. It is, moreover, addressed to the *congregation*, hence the repeated opening clause 'Let us pray for . . .', and the repeated response, which is frequently 'Lord, have mercy'. (Incidentally, it is a pity that responses in the intercessions are not more frequently *sung*.) Alternatively, the petition may well end with 'Let us pray to the Lord', so that the congregation knows when to come in with the response. It is important for the worshipping communities to be familiar and relaxed about their 'cues', because that will enable them to pray the liturgy better.

If the beauty of litanies is their simplicity, it is best to keep the biddings for prayer at approximately the same length and the same style. Thus, there is a tendency to expand on the bidding, to give it a sense of purpose:

'Let us pray for . . . that . . .

Such a developed form is more sophisticated and requires more preparation. It also puts an added strain on the intercessor to make the final clause creatively ambiguous, so that God is not instructed too specifically about what is to happen.

The second type of intercession is a different development of the litany. It consists of a maximum of four elements:

1. bidding for prayer
2. silence
3. versicle and response
4. collect.

Generations of Anglicans know this structure well from the days of Mattins and Evensong, 'after the Third Collect'. The common shape means that the congregation knows the direction of things, and by familiarity with different leaders of intercessions, is likely to know how often the sequence of this liturgical unity is going to be repeated. Usually four or five times is sufficient. But the unit itself is an object lesson in the spirituality of intercession. First of all, the bidding is addressed to the congregation, and it may well be specific in its content, mentioning a local concern, or else a theme from the cycle of prayer used in that community. Then the congregation has the chance to absorb these ideas, and think of others, in the silence that intervenes. Individuals may well go off on their own tangents — that is usually how liturgy and spirituality interconnect. After that, the versicle and response draw thoughts together again. Finally, the collect, addressed to God, sums up the spoken and silent prayers and puts them in general terms, so that different people can relate to them in their own way. The bidding-collect style is still used in the Roman Liturgy on Good Friday and it would be an instructive way of interceding on other occasions too.

The third type of intercession is the form of extended collect that has developed in the Anglican tradition in recent decades at the Eucharist. It begins and ends with the liturgical punctuation marks that are now common coin; an opening clause that sets the scene, and a concluding clause which rounds it off. In the middle, there lies a series of possible alternatives, which include small set paragraphs that focus on prayer for certain common needs; as mentioned previously, these are the Church, secular leaders, the local community, the suffering, the departed, and (though frequently ignored) the saints. The intercessor first has to decide whether or not to use all these topics. The next decision is whether to use the set portions or not. Some people need them, others are so gifted in language that they can well dispense with them. Then the 'ad hoc' prayers have to be written, and here it is important that each is approximately the same length, so that there is a sense of balance and that people listening to the prayers may discern a shape and direction to the prayer. In putting them together, it is also important to make a good balance between 'general' and 'particular', between concerns and interests that will ring immediate bells with some people, and expressing intercessions in more widespread images and terminology that will enable people to use them as they make their own individual petitions silently while the prayer proceeds.

The fourth type of intercession is the extempore form, and this is, for most people, the hardest, because it relies heavily on personal gifts and a religious spirituality that may be more relaxed in a smaller gathering than in a larger public assembly. Even with this kind of prayer, there is usually a shape, and even the most gifted person will have set phrases and favoured mannerisms that either delight ('anoint them with your Spirit') or jar ('we *just* pray'). But in antiquity the standard types of prayer (e.g. the collect, and the eucharistic prayer) began life as prayers that were improvised according to certain norms and shapes. Free kinds of prayer are not the possession of one branch of the Church.

4

In offering intercession, a lot more is going on than appears at first sight, and congregations need to have the hidden power of this essential ingredient in the Eucharist released to them. It is a privilege, and should not be trivialized. It has its proper place, after the Word, and (we hope) at the end of the eucharistic prayer. It has its own rationale, as a crucial means of expressing the interplay of many different relationships, because it focuses on the dialectic of prayer and action. It also takes many forms, and leaders of intercession need to be clear in their minds which form they want to take. Underneath all that, intercession is a solemn, sacrificial activity, which is about the Church offering its very self to the living God, not just in abstract terms that sound good, but in the hard contexts that ordinary Christian men and women have to face day by day. Intercession is, in every sense, a sacrifice that is *reasonable*, which is why it is sometimes referred to as the 'prayer of the faithful', since it is not the disparate thoughts and yearnings of an amorphous group of people, but, rather, the corporate action of the whole Church, sacrificing itself in the service of its Lord.

NOTES

1. See text in R. C. D. Jasper/G. J. Cuming, (ed.), *The Prayers of the Eucharist: Early and Reformed* (New York, Oxford University Press, 1980²), p.90.
2. Geoffrey Wainwright, *Doxology: The Praise of God in Worship, Doctrine and Life* (London, Epworth, 1980), p.355.
3. See Kenneth Stevenson, (ed.), '"Ye Shall Pray For": The Intercession', in Kenneth Stevenson, *Liturgy Reshaped* (London, SPCK, 1982), pp.32–47.
4. Quoted in Stevenson, '"Ye Shall Pray For"', p.33.
5. Anthony Bloom, *Living Prayer* (London, Libra Books, 1966), p.71.
6. See Michael Perham, *Liturgy Pastoral and Parochial* (London, SPCK, 1984), pp.5–7, for an excellent discussion of this.
7. Bernard Levin, *Enthusiasms: An Irresistible Celebration of the Joys of Life* (London, Jonathan Cape, 1983), especially Chapter 1.
8. See Jasper/Cuming, op.cit., pp.36f.

4

SACRIFICE OF THANKS

And for all your graces towards us
let us offer to your glory and honour
in your holy Church before your propitiatory altar.
(Maronite anaphora of Peter the Apostle)[1]

1

The Maronites are a group of ethnic Syrian Christians who have for many centuries worshipped in their own way, with their own traditions, but are also in communion with Rome. In many respects, ecclesiastical, political and social, they are an anomaly. Among the eucharistic prayers which they use is one whose nickname is *sharar*, taken from the opening word in the first paragraph. Although the prayer is ascribed to Peter the Apostle himself (as a pretension towards antiquity), it is unlikely that it goes back that far. But scholars are fascinated by its style and format. Like another Syrian anaphora that has been studied for a long time (ascribed to the Apostles Addai and Mari), this composition probably takes us right back to the Semitic roots of Christianity.

One of the many fruits of liturgical scholarship in this century is the emphasis on the Jewish roots of Christian worship. It suddenly dawned on people that Jesus was a Jew, and that therefore he would have been familiar with the domestic liturgical practices that were developing during his time. Furthermore, the writers of the New Testament were sprung from those roots too. Thus, the New Testament has several passages which may have a liturgical origin, not just the Canticles of Luke's Gospel and the Revelation, but the opening passages of Ephesians and 1 Peter, which begin with the Jewish liturgical code-word, 'Blessed be God . . .',

based on the Jewish *berakah* prayer. The new Roman
Catholic offertory prayers which begin 'Blessed are you,
Lord God of all creation' reflect that penchant for signalling
these Semitic roots in contemporary Christian liturgy.

In the vocabulary of the anaphora of Peter the Apostle are
four important areas of what might be called the psychology
of Christian prayer of thanksgiving at the Lord's Table. The
first is occasioned by the fact that we *offer* God glory and
honour. Unlike English, Syriac has several words that can
be used to express this movement of praise from humanity
to God, and the East Syrian prayers (which include the
aforementioned Addai and Mari) use these terms with
careful nuances. It is not splitting hairs to draw attention to
their variety, because even in the earliest Greek texts that
refer to Christian prayer (e.g. the writings of Justin Martyr),
prayer is not merely verbalized, it is 'sent up' to God.

I do not think that this subtle use of verbs is meant to
draw outmoded pictures of where God is. Rather, it is
intended to express the fact and the experience that when we
stand before God in worship, particularly in solemn
thanksgiving (which is when these words occur with the
greatest frequency), we are offering a spiritual sacrifice, we
are doing something important, something costly, something serious. The language of discourse in worship is
distinct from the kind of conversations that we are likely to
have with each other. That is why from the earliest times,
the eucharistic prayer normally begins with the linguistic
convention that includes 'lift up your hearts'.

The second feature of this prayer is that it refers to the
altar as the focus of Christian worship. Once again, this is a
term deep in the traditional vocabulary of Semitic Christianity. Ignatius of Antioch, no less, uses the word 'altar' to
describe the Christian community, and to be within the altar
is to be in communion with the Church itself.[2] It is more
than probable that Ignatius also means cultic Christian acts,
such as the celebration of the Eucharist – indeed it would be
hard to conclude otherwise. Yet again, the spiritualization of
sacrifice that we noted in the opening chapter is a dominant

feature of the way the first Christians dealt with the apologetic demands laid upon them as a community deriving their existence from a prior religious faith, and therefore needing to show where their own beliefs and practices differed from what they had inherited.

The 'altar' before which glory and honour are offered exemplifies the kind of sacrifice that the Eucharist is. No blood of bulls is offered here. No cereal offerings are consumed. Certainly no human sacrifices are presented. But the 'altar' and the 'offering of glory and honour' are nonetheless *real*. They do not exist just in the mind. Herein lies the principal apologetic problem of the tendency to spiritualize sacrifice. (It corresponds with the problems theologians encounter when they use the word 'myth', because for most people a myth is not true – or real.) The *sharar* makes the bold statement, shortly after the Sanctus, as in our quotation, that the people of God do have an altar.

The third feature is related to the previous one, and it centres around the interpretation of the expression 'propitiatory altar'. Here once again we have creative ambiguity. There can be no sense in which the table of the Eucharist of its own accord becomes 'propitiatory'. The clue comes from the Sanctus itself, where the Church joins in the worship of heaven. That being the case, the Sanctus just having been sung, then the 'altar' which is 'propitiatory' is, surely, the altar of God in heaven, which the eucharistic table symbolizes.

This is, perhaps, the hardest notion of all, because the idea of earthly and heavenly worship being united is not popular in much contemporary worship. Like the saints, heaven somehow misses out. But the notion of heaven on earth is closely linked to the fact that Christ is made available to all who believe in him; hence the image of his intercession for us at the right hand of the Father.

The fourth feature, which is reflected more in the whole drift of the prayer rather than in the quotation, can be discerned in the way in which prayers of this type handle the history of salvation in its entirety. Modern eucharistic prayers rehearse the mighty acts of God in various ways. The 'story' of the Christian faith is not read in Scripture, as it was earlier in the liturgy, but now becomes a kind of incantation, which is one of the reasons why eucharistic prayers are frequently chanted, making the point that it is a type of prayer quite different in function from any other in the service. How is this salvation history handled?

There are two axes.[3] One axis may be called the *vertical*. In this, the emphasis is on what God has done. Thus, salvation history may be a rich, full catalogue of creation, the calling of the patriarchs, the prophets, the sending of Jesus as incarnate Word, his life and ministry, and his death and resurrection. Even though many modern prayers resemble one another in both subject and style (because similar models have been employed in their construction), the permutations inherent in this kind of ground plan are almost limitless. A prayer can have a particular theological slant within this 'vertical' axis. God's mighty acts can be seen in terms of creation and new creation, redemption and cross, covenant and renewal.

The second axis is the *horizontal*. In this, the emphasis properly lies on the life of the community and its appropriation of these mighty acts. Thus, the response of the people of God to redemptive acts, whether in the calling of the prophets or the ministry of Jesus, takes a high profile. Moreover, when the prayer moves into those portions which deal with the life of the Church, the accent falls on what the Christian community thinks it is doing at the Eucharist.

History is full of examples of prayers such as the *sharar* itself in which these two dimensions mix happily together, in the interests of balance. History also knows many prayers in which the vertical axis is so dominant that the horizontal appears to be inactive, and contrariwise there are also prayers that are so horizontal in their scope that the vertical appears incidental.

Many modern compositions seem to be unable to hold a constructive balance. Official texts appear vertically-orientated, almost to the extent that God is thanked for a whole series of primeval actions, for which there are a few results, if the Christian community happens to want them. On the other hand, many an *ad hoc* anaphora revels in the sin and dejection of the contemporary world, to the extent that we get no further than to look at our own tiny existence; there is no beyond.

Can these four features serve our generation? Not by some trick of archaism, because our own climate is a different one. But they could resurface, in terms that match our experience. We need to inculcate a sense of sacrifice in liturgical speech, because we live in a world that mistrusts words. Expressions of community, both worldwide and heavenward, could offset current tendencies towards eucharistic introspection. Certainly contemporary interest in history, roots, and antiquity demonstrates a basic desire to come to terms with what has gone before us. And prayers that manage to express the nature of Godhead in human experience in a vertical–horizontal manner could perhaps serve to build up pieties that are more wholesome.

2

The tension between vertical and horizontal can also conceal further obstacles that are to do with the accessibility of the past. Can the post-Enlightenment age relate properly to traditional concepts of these 'mighty acts'? Earlier this century, Gregory Dix, who probably did more to popularize the study and understanding of liturgy than anyone else in our time, attempted to get round this problem by reviving the primitive notion of anamnesis in a Jewish-inspired way, that links the eucharistic celebration of Christ with the Jewish celebration(*zikkaron*) of the Passover. We bring before God his great actions in the past in such a way that their consequences have effect *now*.[4]

Such a view is allied to a strongly Catholic view of sacramental efficacy. It tends to read into Jewish liturgical practice a somewhat 'higher' view of what they are doing than they would actually say themselves! More helpful, perhaps, is an anthropological view that sees Christians as people who become part of a tradition by entering into it. As the German writer Hans-Georg Gadamer has aptly put, 'History does not belong to us, we belong to it.'[5] One of the ways of expressing this 'belonging' is to enter into it through the symbolic activity of worship, building up our sense of continuity with the past, but within the tradition, being able to perceive new ways of appropriating God's grace. The trouble with Dix's view is that it can so easily be caricatured; turn the clock back to antiquity and all will be well, especially if it is backed up by a medieval Latin view of how sacraments operate.

The best movements in the Church are often those which understand the background, the context, in which change can take place. Our ways of thinking today are necessarily pluralistic, and our liturgies have to carry much more variety than we often realize: variety of background, education, work, family life-style and relationships. A case in point for liturgy is the work of the Liturgical Commission of the Church of England in discussing possible eucharistic prayers for use in Urban Priority Areas. This raises all kinds of issues. On the one hand, we do not want to treat these parishes in such a different category that they are patronized, and have special liturgies imposed on them from above. On the other hand, they *are* so distinct that the liturgies of the Alternative Service Book need adaptation before they are used there.

In writing eucharistic prayers with these communities in mind, we have first to experience their kind of life, and then their kind of worship. We have to listen to their thoughts, the way they relate to their environment. We have to identify which images of the Christian faith are most vivid to them. Among the surprises of this Pandora's Box are the following:

1. An interest in the life of the local community long before the present housing was set up, as well as in the place of their own ethnic community before they came to this country.

2. A concern for human rights, and the relationship between those who live in the community and those who come from outside to work among them.

3. Because they are the church of the poor, the crucifixion is the sign of the suffering Christ. If they do not get the cross in their prayer, they will bring it out in their piety, and hymnody.

4. Because their style of worship blends 'Catholic' and 'Evangelical' in sometimes demonstrative ways, many of them are naturally suspicious of liberal reasonableness, what has been described as 'poker-faced liturgy'.

5. As many of the studies of Latin-American Liberation Theology show, they identify more easily with stories of redemption in the Bible.

From these undercurrents (and there are many others that could be mentioned), certain basic themes emerge about eucharistic spirituality. Much of it is covered by the all-embracing word 'ambience'. Every community must worship in its own way and make its own mark on its own building. But there is much more to it than that.

So far from needing a prayer that celebrates their own life as if it were a life of its own, they want prayers that link them to the rest of humanity worldwide (as witness their own ethnic wanderings) and history-deep (as witness their own environmental changes). Because many of them are the church of the poor, in every sense, they want images of Christ which identify with poverty, but at the same time point to his riches, not in a contrived way (a 'happy ending' Christology), but in a way that is truly paradoxical. As lovers of story, their prayer must have a sense of *narrative* about it, with a bit of light and shade, particularly in the way that the story of Jesus Christ is told. Finally, in the Eucharist, the Lucan image of Jesus sitting down to eat with sinners is a particularly fruitful motif. A community of this sort at worship wants to say that the Eucharist celebrates the values of the Kingdom, and indeed inaugurates it.

How is all this put into words? Inspired by the 'vertical-horizontal' theme, such a prayer could move on from the Sanctus in the following way:

> How wonderful the work of your hands, O Lord!
> As a mother tenderly gathers her children
> you embraced a people as your own.
> From them you raised up Jesus, our Saviour,
> born of Mary, to be the living bread,
> in whom all our hungers are satisfied.[6]

This can be compared with the corresponding passage in *sharar* for style and approach rather than content:

> We give thanks to you, O Lord,
> we your sinful servants
> because you have effected in us your grace
>   which cannot be repaid.
> You put on our humanity so as to quicken us by your
>   divinity.
> You lifted up our poverty and righted our dejection.
> And you quickened our mortality, and you justified
>   our sinfulness and you forgave our debts.
> And you enlightened our understanding and
>   vanquished our enemies
> and made triumphant our lowliness.
> And for all your graces towards us . . .[7]

Some of the official texts which have been produced in the new service books somehow miss out on these wide anthropological musings which are also strongly christocentric. If the next step were to write prayers that reached out for some of these thoughts and feelings, many of the criticisms of the anaphoras in current use might be met in full measure. Many an official text is found by congregations to be overlong, and length is not always relieved by the inclusion of repeated congregational responses in a prayer sometimes criticized for being a priestly monologue. Perhaps these faults are part and parcel of having had to produce new prayers rapidly.

But where does this leave us in relation to salvation

history as *history*? It means, primarily, that prayer-writing has to hold together godward and humanward, vertical and horizontal, and that the images used need to have a paradoxical ring about them, rather than a neat and logical piece of biblical plasticine. It also means that it is going to be impossible for a eucharistic prayer to contain everything. It is therefore better to have a short eucharistic prayer that is direct in power and selective in its material than a lengthy composition that tries to put all the goods of Christianity into the front of the shop-window. In any case, long prayers are the most difficult to put togethert because their juncture points are most obvious, and because they need to be held together by an inner coherence that is not always easy to achieve. The various versions of the anaphora of Basil of Caesarea demonstrate this clearly; the earliest text travels through a longer intermediary before emerging in the fulsome version used today on special occasions in the Byzantine Church. Unlike the Bible, the liturgy does not have canonical status. Although it is usually a conservative business, it does change, and when it changes, it tends to work hard in order to be receptive to the brainstorm that has been causing the changes to happen.

When it comes to the eucharistic prayer, history is full of answers to the questions of how the rendering of thanks to God can be expressed within the conventions of liturgical prayer. In the Eastern Churches, there are single eucharistic prayers, that do not have any variety within them. For example, the Byzantine rite employs three anaphoras, though in practice only two are used with regularity. These are the anaphora of Basil of Caesarea (on solemn days) and that of John Chrysostom (on other occasions). The Syrian Orthodox Church has no fewer than seventy anaphoras, though the bulk of them are rarely used. But once upon a time, different prayers were used with frequency and the communities which used them could cope with that variety by the simple expedient of knowing what shape the prayers took.

In a previous chapter, we outlined the logic of the

standard Eastern pattern: praise for creation, leading into Sanctus; thanksgiving for redemption, in the Old Covenant, and in the work of Christ; the Institution Narrative; and the act of remembrance (anamnesis) and prayer for the Holy Spirit (epiclesis); this leads into intercessions for the living and departed; and the whole prayer is rounded off in a doxology, to reaffirm that it is only in Christ and through Christ that we are able to render praise and glory to God. Such a shape has a commendable beauty about it. It has served as the model for many modern compositions, whether those which insert a 'split' epiclesis (Roman Missal 1970 and Alternative Service Book 1980), or those which stick to the Eastern structure more faithfully (Scottish Episcopal from 1764 onwards and American Episcopal from 1789 onwards).

The medieval West, however, adopted a different way of handling variety which was more sensitive to the liturgical year. Whereas the Eastern texts celebrate the whole of salvation history on every occasion, the West soon developed variety within the prayer itself. In the Roman rite, the portion of the prayer from the opening dialogue to the introduction to the Sanctus (the *praefatio* or 'preface') began to vary according to set norms when the Latin service-books were developing. The growth of the Proper Preface developed in conjunction with the liturgical year and with the local needs of the Eucharist, as it began to accommodate itself to a new environment in the Middle Ages, namely being celebrated at a side altar, with no communicants, and being offered for all sorts of concerns.

The Roman prayer, unlike the Eastern prayers, moves straight into supplication after the Sanctus, with a series of petitions for the acceptance of the offering. The old Latin books frequently make provision for one of these prayers (the *Hanc igitur*) to vary also, according to the occasion. (There are a few of these in the 1970 Missal.) Thus, both liturgical time and pastoral context find expression in the Church's thank-offering prayer. It it interesting to note that, unlike the Eastern texts, which are single items in themselves, the Roman tradition allows variation to be focused on the two deep structures of the eucharistic prayer, namely thanksgiving (Preface) and supplication (*Hanc igitur*).

However, in the old Spanish and Frankish rites, which were eventually replaced by the Roman rite during the Middle Ages, a slightly different system operated. According to these venerable liturgies, the eucharistic prayer was constructed according to a common ground-plan, but the variable paragraphs were much longer, whether they were part of the thanksgiving series, or whether they made up the 'anamnesis' section (after the Institution Narrative). Particularly in the Spanish books, these prayers wax eloquent on salvation history and the meaning of the Eucharist in its seasonal context; for example, Lamb-imagery abounds at Easter.

In the modern Western service-books, however, the thanksgiving series varies in yet another way. It either remains fixed, as in Roman Eucharistic Prayer IV, or it is possible to introduce variable sections in a Proper Preface, as in Roman Eucharistic Prayers II and III, and those of other Churches. Such a compromise has its weaknesses, particularly when, in a short prayer, there may be a Proper Preface which expands on a feature mentioned later on.

Such a concern with the liturgical year, the calendar, and also with pastoral context, is an example of the difference between Eastern and Western Christianity. In the East, to ritualize the changes of the year within the great prayer of the Church was not a felt need. In the West, by contrast, the prayer is adapted, so that it is made up of various building-bricks, particularly in the old Spanish tradition, all fitted into one prayer. And behind this love of variety is a sensitivity to the eucharistic prayer as being at root a prayer of thanksgiving and supplication. Such a sensitivity too often seems lacking today.

The new prayers made a bold step forward. Before 1970, the Roman rite had many fewer Proper Prefaces, and much less emphasis on creation, a subject both traditional and of very modern concern to ordinary men and women. Similarly, the Book of Common Prayer, confined thanking God for creation to the General Thanksgiving, which has nothing to do with the eucharistic liturgy, it was so sixteenth-century in its theological priorities that, apart from in the Creed, the resurrection of Christ was mentioned in the Eucharist at Easter, no more. The new service-books have brought with them incalculable gains. It is for us, therefore, to grasp at three opportunities.

The first is to understand more fully what those thanksgivings are actually saying, and not regard them just as verbiage to which we must become accustomed. This can be done partly by praying them apart from the liturgy. It can also be done by a more imaginative choice of hymnody to point up seasonal concerns. It can be achieved by more flexibility within the choice of texts: for example, on Remembrance Sunday, the preacher might quote an Easter Preface, a very appropriate use of it in the eucharistic prayer at that celebration.

The second is to be aware of the 'vertical-horizontal' dialectic at work in the prayer, particularly as that dialectic is in itself a paradigm of the redemptive work that we can, in our more tragic or glorious moments, perceive within ourselves. We send up praise and thanksgiving to God, rendering the Christian story in poetic form, but we only do this as a solemn sacrificial activity because of God's prior commitment to us. Some prayers are more successful in this regard than others and it is to be hoped that they will stand the test of time.

The third is to deepen our sensitivity to the quality of the tradition we have entered into. The past owns us, and many are the people who will flock into ancient buildings in order to explore their own and other people's roots, seeking a communion with the past to counterbalance the discontinuities of their everyday life. Some of the broad images of anaphoras, both old and new, may help us to engage in that exercise, not as an act of self-indulgence but as a means of moving on to the future.

Iris Murdoch's novel, *The Good Apprentice*,[8] exemplifies this spiritual progression. Her quasi-hero, Edward Baltram, begins the book shattered by a feeling of responsibility for the death of a friend. At the end of the book, he drinks to the future. But he only gets there by going on a weird and wonderful pilgrimage in the course of which he comes to terms with himself and his past, and discovers how best he can take the next step in his life. Perhaps he becomes a little less earnest and by the last page he comes across as lilting a bit more. The transformation is not total. Nonetheless, the book, coming as it does from a secular tradition of spiritual comment, is a warning to the Church to keep perspectives on our past and our roots seriously, and not become too dismissive of them. To offer glory and honour to God on his propitiatory altar in heaven is to set ourselves the task of seeing all of history – our own tiny bits of it included – under the gaze of eternity. And that is the home where it properly belongs.

NOTES

1. See text in Bryan D. Spinks, *Addai and Mari – The Anaphora of the Apostles: A Text for Students*, Grove Liturgical Study 24 (Bramcote, Grove, 1980), p.17.
2. See Rowan Williams, *Eucharistic Sacrifice – The Roots of a Metaphor*, Grove Liturgical Study 31 (Bramcote, Grove, 1982), pp.18ff.
3. I owe much of this discussion to J. M. Sánchez Caro, *Eucaristía e Historia de la Salvación* (Madrid, La Editorial Católica, 1983).
4. Gregory Dix, *The Shape of the Liturgy* (London, Dacre, 1945), p.161. See also Kenneth Stevenson, *Gregory Dix 25 Years On*, Grove Liturgical Study 10 (Bramcote, Grove, 1977), p.26.
5. Quoted by Andrew Louth in 'The Nature of Theological Understanding: some parallels between Newman and Gadamer', in Geoffrey Rowell, ed., *Tradition Renewed: The Oxford Movement Conference Papers* (London, Darton, Longman & Todd, 1986), p.102.
6. Text drafted for the Church of England Liturgical Commission.
7. See Spinks, p.17.
8. Iris Murdoch, *The Good Apprentice* (London, Penguin, 1986).

5

PRESENTS?

⚜

Therefore, master, we also, remembering his life-giving Cross,
his three-day burial, his resurrection from the dead, his ascension
into heaven, his enthronement at your right hand, God the
Father, and his glorious and fearful second coming;
bringing you your own, from your own, in all and through
all . . .

(Liturgy of St Basil)[1]

1

It is now over twenty years since the Church of England
Liturgical Commission attempted a drastic revision of its
eucharistic prayer and the controversy that ensued centred
round this paragraph. It is a crucial section of the prayer, to
be sure, because of the place that it occupies. It is central,
because it expresses what the Eucharist is supposed to do.
It is sensitive, because of the issues that it raises about
eucharistic doctrine. In the end, a compromise was reached,
and, with little substantial change, that compromise re-
mained in force throughout the production of the prayers as
they appear in the Alternative Service Book of 1980. What is
all the fuss about?

At root, it is about whether or not the act of remembering
Jesus at the Lord's Supper involves offering the bread and
wine to God. On the one side, those with Reformation sensitivities refuse to touch any language of offering, because
that smacks of the medieval Mass. On the other side, there
are many who would describe themselves as loyal to the
Reformation but who do not fear such language, because the
simple logic of the prayer suggests that movement of ideas;
thanksgiving leads into supplication (like the Jewish table

prayers), and when that supplication is about to ask for the descent of the Spirit on the Eucharist, the gifts of bread and wine should, surely, be referred to in terms that imply that they are being presented before God.

At first sight, the controversy seems a very domestic Church of England matter. But the issues raised by this debate are much wider, because they are about how far Reformation Churches are prepared to readmit language of sacrifice that they eschewed so vehemently in the sixteenth century, and about how far the Roman Catholic Church may be deemed to have redressed the balance by widening its own eucharistic vocabulary in the prayers of the Missal of 1970.

There *are* many Reformation Churches that have done just that. The Anglican liturgies of Scotland, the USA, Canada, South Africa, and many others have long opted for the offering language of sacrifice, albeit circumscribed. The hymns of the Wesleys betray a richness of expression that would have been unthinkable a century or two before. Nonetheless, in the words of Paul Bradshaw, referring to the 1967 controversy, many Evangelicals 'were unable to ignore the doctrinal water which had flowed under the liturgical bridge'.[2] Before we return to this matter, it is necessary to set the historical record straight. There is nothing 'normative' about the expression 'remembering . . . we offer'. As we have shown in a detailed study of this complex matter,[3] the term first appears in the anaphora that is to be found in the *Apostolic Tradition* of Hippolytus, which probably dates from the early third century, and may reflect the use of the Church of Rome. This prayer has had a great influence on many recent compositions of the Western Churches. Indeed, it could be said that its influence on the twentieth century far outstrips its influence on the third and fourth! This very part of the prayer, which remembers the work of Christ, was probably inserted into the earlier form of the anaphora with the Institution Narrative. The evolution may be summarized thus:

Pristine form	*Later form*
Thanksgiving series - - - - -	Thanksgiving series
(work of Christ)	(creation, work of Christ)
	Institution Narrative
	Anamnesis
Supplication- - - - - - - - - -	Supplication
(Spirit on the Eucharist)	(Spirit on the Eucharist,
	Intercessions)

Such, it would seem, was how the standard Eastern shape of the prayer developed. But even that is to simplify things, because it gives the impression that we possess all the Eastern prayers that have ever been used.

Two important exceptions have to be noted at this point. One is the eucharistic prayer of St Mark (once the standard prayer of the Coptic Church but now rarely used). In this prayer, the shape is somewhat different, and the language of sacrifice uses a past tense ('we presented') at the anamnesis, as if referring back to an already completed action. The other exception that we know in detail is that maverick of antiquity mentioned in an earlier chapter, the anaphora of Addai and Mari, which is used by the Nestorians and the Malabar Catholics. This prayer is more Semitic than any other, but the important feature is that it probably never originally contained the Institution Narrative at all, so that it does not contain an anamnesis section. Its language of offering is bold, simple and unitive, for in it the whole Eucharist is offered, and the Spirit is asked to descend on the offering of the Church (meaning the whole Eucharist).

Neither Copts nor Nestorians, nor (for that matter) Malabar Catholics hold some special insight into the Eucharist that places them in a position of pre-eminence. But there are important theological conclusions to draw from such a variety in the Christian story. It is important for modern Westerners, who are trying to heal the sad divisions of the Reformation era, to take in the simplicity and variations that gave rise to these different texts, many of which are still used today.

When we look at the other Eastern Churches, the picture becomes fuller still. For both the Armenians and the Syrian Jacobites tend to refrain from offering the gifts in remembrance of Christ. Frequently, in the anamnesis, the prayer moves on with an urgent sweep that takes in the Christ event in extended, rhetorical fashion, but the actual language is usually 'we commemorate', not 'we offer'. In this tradition, the more 'unitive' view of eucharistic sacrifice reappears, so that it is not the gifts that are offered, but the whole Lord's Supper, as a sacrifice of thanks and praise. In the epiclesis, when the Spirit is prayed for, the gifts are often referred to as oblations. But the whole feel of this tradition is distinct, and it needs to be noted.

In fact the expression 'remembering . . . we offer' is but a linguistic convention that appears in the eucharistic prayers of the Byzantine rite, and also the old Roman Canon (Eucharistic Prayer I in the 1970 Missal). When the rest of the East is balanced out, we see a wider view of offering, and the actual words used vary considerably. It is important to see this richness for what it is. For at the very time when (some might claim) the sacrificial terminology might have become distinctly up-market (that is, when the local liturgies were developing from the fourth century onwards), the words of sacrifice are, in fact, words of presentation and commemoration.

The Roman Canon, however, is a different animal. Because since 1970 it has been but one prayer among four (and, when others have been authorized, the choice is widened further), it is difficult for us to imagine the impact of that prayer being repeated, again and again, as the sole eucharistic prayer of one of the largest groups of Christians in the world. In a previous chapter, we noted its proclivity for variety in the two traditional 'deep structures' of the eucharistic prayer, namely thanksgiving (the Proper Preface) and supplication (the *Hanc igitur*). The principal feature of the prayer, however, is its emphasis on offering and sacrifice throughout the second part. To hear it read aloud reveals how the language of offering dominates, from after the Sanctus and Benedictus to the concluding doxology.

The trouble is that the Canon has suffered from being misunderstood. The Reformers knew it well and saw it in the pastoral setting of the silent Mass, with few, or no, communicants. Not knowing its background, they failed to understand why it emerged in the way that it did. Some of them, including Melanchthon, knew the Byzantine prayers, and regarded them as preferable because of the circum-scribed way that they handle sacrifice and offering. But the Canon's preoccupation with sacrifice may well have resulted from a desire to widen the concept, and that is something to be avoided. It is much more important to unravel history in order to understand it better than to try to ape a past age without realizing the many forces (not just liturgical) that made it what it was.

Returning, now, to the controversy, what can history say? First of all, history gives us no norms. Rather, history gives us an almost bewildering variety. The Roman Canon says, 'we offer, we offer, accept our offering'. The Byzan-tine prayers say, 'remembering his death . . ., we present . . .'. The Armenians and West Syrians say, earlier in the prayer, 'we offer praise and thanksgiving', but often only say at this point, 'we commemorate'. And so the variety goes on.

Second, the variety indicates that it is likely to go on throughout Christian history, as communities work out their own ways of handling the inner movements of the Eucharist, which are about offering thanks to God and about asking him to bless the gathering of his people around the Lord's Table.

Third, it should also help Reformation Christians, particu-larly as they look at the East, to see that it *is* possible to use liturgies that express the spiritualization of sacrifice. We ought to be able to 'offer thanks and praise', and, surely, we ought to be able to refer to the gifts of bread and wine in direct terms when we offer the memorial. It is interesting that the word 'bring' appears in the third of the Eucharistic Prayers of the Alternative Service Book. That very neutrality of expression is similarly to be found in some of the prayers of antiquity.

Fourth, when Churches engage in ecumenical dialogue, they should look further afield than to their own particular liturgical texts in searching for accord. It would do ARCIC good to take stock of how matters of eucharistic theology find expression in the Eastern texts, many of which are actually used by Catholics of the Eastern rites themselves.[4]

Finally, because history gives no direct norms, we should become more sensitive to the circumspect way in which many of these formulations have evolved down the ages, and also to when and where the seeds of later mistakes have been sown. If the Roman Canon had only been given some alternatives in 570 instead of 1970, it is conceivable that some of the trouble that came to a head at the Reformation might not have been so severe. Liturgies need a pastoral and doctrinal critique, not least while they are being brought to birth.

2

History is a useful antidote to the preoccupations of the twentieth century with questions about remembrance and offering. It is no less an ally when we turn to the question of what is meant when the bread and wine are placed on the altar.

Once again, this is an issue about which Reformation sensitivities are repeatedly raised, and the Reformation liturgies are almost an object-lesson in the strength of reaction against the offertory at that time. But the background is, once again, important.

In the Middle Ages, the priest would recite a whole series of private prayers while the gifts of bread and wine were being prepared and placed on the altar immediately prior to the eucharistic prayer. At the time of the Canon's definitive text (about the fifth–sixth century), the Roman rite had *one* prayer that was used just before the eucharistic prayer, and it would vary with the season and day, together with the collect and the post-communion. Originally, such a prayer was framed in general terms, about the presentation of gifts, though even here it often lacked direct reference to the bread and wine. It served the function of summarizing all the preparatory character of the Mass up to that point. But as time went on, and as the pastoral orientation of the Mass became more private (with the move from basilica to side-altar), and as the priest himself (rather than other ministers) did the preparing, additional, fixed prayers were composed locally, so that the priest had something to say all the time while performing the liturgical actions of preparation. These prayers frequently took up the theme of offering and sometimes they even expanded on ideas from the Canon. Some localities, such as Salisbury, were reticent, short, restrained. Others, such as the monasteries, were expansive, repetitive, fulsome.

The Reformers would have been aware of these texts – Martin Luther would have known by heart those of his own religious house. The very fact that they were variations on one theme would only serve to underline the need to get rid of them.

But you can only successfully get rid of something in the liturgy if you replace it with something else. It is therefore almost whimsical that in the Book of Common Prayer, the liturgical action which takes place in the part of the eucharistic rite corresponding to the presentation of the gifts is the collection. Perhaps this was the 'Christmas game' to which the people of Cornwall objected when the 1549 rite was first used among them.[5] Nonetheless, the taking of the collection soon etched itself into the corporate consciousness of the tradition. Many people today cannot even think of any service taking place without the collection! Moreover, when the final touches were being put to the Prayer Book before its production in 1662, the money was directed to be presented *at the holy table*.

The trouble is that in the intervening centuries the custom has grown up of making a fuss both of the presentation of cash and of the eucharistic gifts. Sidespersons have for long regarded it as their privilege and ministry to handle the money and there are occasions when, particularly in our great cathedrals, this part of the offertory is given such solemnity that the priest elevates the alms-dish in a way strongly reminiscent of the old elevations of bread and wine in the Mass. Similarly, earlier this century the custom grew up of 'the offertory procession', whereby laypersons carry up the bread and wine in a little procession, to symbolize that they are providing the eucharistic gifts themselves. Often this was exactly the case: there are congregations in which families appear in rota to bake the bread, and sometimes to provide the wine.

Once again, history comes to our aid, on two counts. First of all, many of the Eastern prayers contain intercessions for those who have offered the gifts of bread and wine, as if to express a desire to associate the offerers with the whole celebration. If, as was usually the case, the bread and wine at the altar had been chosen from various gifts presented by the people before the service began, to pray for those responsible for providing the eucharistic gifts is a legitimate development. In the 'offertory procession' in our own day, we see a variation of this trend. If you associate people with a given liturgical action, you involve them with the Eucharist at a deep level.

Second, in the Byzantine rite, there is an elaborate procession of the gifts in the middle of the Liturgy, called the 'Great Entrance'. (This is to distinguish it from the 'Little Entrance' earlier in the rite, when the Gospel Book is solemnly taken to the altar for the start of the Liturgy of the Word.) This 'Great Entrance' is performed exclusively by clergy, and it is accompanied by much pomp. In popular piety, the as yet unconsecrated gifts are treated as if they were already consecrated. And yet the prayers and chants that accompany this action are all preparatory in character. Even though the *actions* make this procession look like an offertory, the *texts* all look forward to the consecration. Is there a lesson here? The lesson is about a theme we have already touched upon – paradox. There is not one single offertory rite that does not contain some element of paradox, either in the texts themselves, or in the aspirations of those who carry them out. There is a general desire to make something of the action of placing the gifts on the table, but there is also a cautionary feeling that not too much should be said, because either it will say things about that action which are too strong and pretentious, or else what is said will anticipate the eucharistic prayer.

The Roman rite of 1970 contains a much-simplified offertory rite, which includes those new Jewish-inspired prayers, 'Blessed are you, Lord God of all creation'. But it also includes a particularly problematic feature that high-lights the Reformation dispute. In the little dialogue, 'Pray, my brothers and sisters', the priest expresses his relationship with the congregation in terms that are not consonant with much of what we are trying to say about the role of the eucharistic president in the twentieth century. The very words, 'your sacrifice and mine', give rise to all sorts of con-fusion, because it is not clear whether the sacrifice is 'mine' (i.e. primarily the priest's), or 'yours also' (i.e. the Eucharist is the people's offering and the priest is there to preside).

The 1970 text is more restrained than the 1570 Missal at this point, but it is a pity that the dialogue was not omitted altogether (it did not appear in the 1965 draft 'Missa normativa' at all). Many Anglicans feel the need to use it, as an emblem of catholicity. But because the relationship it expresses is so unhelpful, and not conducive to the wider view of offering that we are trying to expound in this book, it would be better if it were left out altogether, as an unnecessary relic of the medieval Mass. But the questions that it raises are important ones for eucharistic theology because they are about the relationship between the presi-dent and the people. When the priest says 'Lift up your hearts', the signal is given that a particularly important part of the liturgy is about to begin. The dialogue is, therefore, really about mutuality of relationships; the president cannot proceed without the assembly's assent. But if the priest says, 'Pray my brothers and sisters that your sacrifice and mine may be acceptable to God the Almighty Father', the congregation which replies in terms of the sacrifice being acceptable at the *hands* of the priest is surely saying something more than acknowledging the leadership that the priest exercises in the service. It reads a little like a restrictive practices code of a Trade Union.

At the other end of the spectrum, the American *Lutheran Book of Worship* (1978) contains a prayer for use at the presentation of the gifts that strikes the right note of paradox, and aptly expands the Roman original, though it is somewhat verbose as a preparatory prayer:

> Blessed are you, O Lord our God, maker of all things.
> Through your goodness you have blessed us with these
>   gifts.
> With them we offer ourselves to your service
> and dedicate our lives to the care and redemption of all
> that you have made, for the sake of him who gave himself
>   for us,
> Jesus Christ our Lord.[6]

Self-oblation, which will figure in the next chapter, is a sobering corrective to any sense of having something to offer to God. Beneath all the verbal posturing in the Reformation debate, the two sides differ in attitude. Catholics think that they *can* stand before God with something to present to him, whereas many Protestants want to emphasize that it is thanks to God's goodness that we have them in the first place. And yet this latter message is precisely what the new Roman Jewish-inspired texts have to say. Perhaps we are not so far apart after all. The popular acclamation, 'Yours, Lord', is intended to refer only to the offering of cash, though most congregations interpret it as a reference to the bread and wine as well, an unfortunate Anglican muddle, which only serves to point up the unsatisfactory character of modern offertory rites.

3

We can now return to the present day, somewhat better

informed about the complexity of the tradition to which many of us are heirs. Traditions, as we have had cause to point out, are not normative. There is no point in perpetuating what was done in the past if it makes no sense whatever in the present. History is full of occasions when our forebears have adopted one of two courses when faced with the need to change. They have either *added* new material to the liturgy in a style and language that expressed what they wanted to say in a way that suited them. This is what happened in the Middle Ages with all those offertory prayers, and it is also what took place when the Wesley eucharistic hymns appeared, to supplement Cranmer's Communion rite with devotional verses of a different and more high-church character.

Alternatively, they have sought to *excise* the unwanted material and put in its place new elements. This is probably what happened when the old Roman Canon was being put together. It is certainly what took place at the Western Reformation. Luther, Calvin, Zwingli and Cranmer all had their liturgical programmes, which they carried out with varying degrees of liturgical conservatism.

In our century, in the interests of restoring what has been lost, the process of innovation has been carried further. We now speak of a single entity, the eucharistic prayer, and encourage congregations to remain standing throughout, even confronting that gut-reaction on the part of people who want to kneel down after the Sanctus because they feel in their bones that the prayer is changing gear into something solemn and sacred. We have composed prayers based on ancient models, but have included twentieth-century concerns, such as creation and ecology, reconciliation and justice, and we therefore often depict Jesus in the stark terms of the Gospels, rather than in the glorified forms found in some of the older liturgies.

In the opening chapter, we quoted two examples of the modern anamnesis, first the Roman Eucharistic Prayer IV ('We offer you his body and blood'), and then the third Eucharistic Prayer from the Alternative Service Book ('We bring before you this bread and this cup'). What criticisms can now be made of these formulations?

The Roman Catholic text is unfortunate, for reasons that we can now enumerate. The whole tenor of that prayer is based on the Coptic version of the anaphora of Basil of Caesarea. When it was decided to use this as a model, the study-group charged with writing the new eucharistic prayers that were to appear in the 1970 Missal regarded this as an ecumenical gesture of unity with the Eastern Churches. (Versions of the Basil of Caesarea prayer are used by Byzantines, Copts, Armenians and Syrians, so they could hardly have chosen a more fitting tradition from which to make such a gesture.) But nowhere in any of these versions does the Eucharist go anywhere near saying that in remembering the work of Christ the Church 'offers his body and blood'. Such a high view of eucharistic sacrifice may well accord with the piety of some traditional Catholics in the West in the intervening centuries, but to foist such an interpretation on to a text that is commendably reticent on the issue is not only to seem to 'correct' it but to provide another, quite avoidable, ecumenical stumbling-block. The Basil texts in their Eastern versions 'present' the gifts – they never 'offer' Christ's Body and Blood.

The Church of England formulation is less unsatisfactory, because it says what many within the tradition think the eucharistic prayer is doing. Moreover, in opting for the neutral word 'present' the compilers have shown commendable restraint, avoiding sensitive terms like 'offer'. But the trouble with the expression is that it appears in isolation in the prayer, for the key, surely, is that the 'bringing' should be linked closely *either* with the 'remembering', *or* (better still) with the 'praying' for the Spirit. Other Anglican rites, such as that of the American Episcopal Church, manage to put the language of offering both in the wider context of sacrifice and in the act of remembrance. Thus, one of the prayers in the 1979 Book of Common Prayer runs as follows:

And we offer our sacrifice of praise and thanksgiving to you, O Lord of all; presenting to you, from your own creation, this bread and this wine.[7]

The beauty of such a formulation is that it has the right element of paradox and it contrasts God's essential gifts with the action of the Church and at the same time brings them together. The whole thanksgiving of the Eucharist is offered, because that is the sacrifice. The gifts are presented only, because they are only a part of the totality of the sacrifice.

Other modern examples can be found. Many of them build on the notion of dynamic memorial that has fed so much twentieth-century ecumenical agreement. The dividing line between Catholics and Protestants is much less pronounced than it has been. The problems occur when formulations have to be found to express what the Church is doing with the bread and wine. Many of us are happy with the language of offering, but others avoid it because of Reformation sensitivities. But I would plead for a wider appreciation of the language of paradox (which is not the same as compromise) as one of the keys to this problem.

What of the offertory? It has never been an entirely coherent or happy ingredient in the liturgy, as it has suffered from various diseases, such as anticipation, exaggeration, strong language, and overdefinition. In our day, there seems to be a felt need to express something of our dependence upon God in bringing the fruits of the earth within the sacramental orbit of his grace. There have been distinguished efforts to delineate clearly between prayers over money and prayers over bread and wine in this act of preparation. How such distinctions are perceived by ordinary people is hard to tell.

Perhaps the best way forward is to recognize this need – but not to take it too seriously. Protestants are often too sensitive about the question of appearing to earn grace by religious action (the charge of being Pelagian). Catholics, perhaps, need to lose their confidence in coming before God repeatedly in commemorating Christ. We all stand in need of God's grace, and when nature and grace are brought together, as in the Eucharist, words of preparation are perhaps only secondary.

Max Thurian has written:

> When the Church has gathered everything together to present it to God, it realizes its utter poverty; all it can do is to put this utter poverty into the hands of Christ who, taking it up into his own sacrifice presented in intercession, makes it a true praise, an efficacious prayer, a valid sacrifice, 'through him, with him and in him'.[8]

But one more cautionary note needs to be sounded, for it strikes at the very heart of both the language of and the motive for offering. The language of propitiation is notoriously difficult to handle, because in the popular mind it conjures up images of Christ placating an angry God. This is a notion easily transmuted to a eucharistic rite which is understood to be in any sense 'propitiatory'. David Power[9] has recently studied the development of sacrifice in the Latin tradition, and has demonstrated that more central to that tradition is the view that the sacrifice of the Eucharist is one of *suffrage*, rather than propitiation. In other words, we come before God with our gifts, pleading the work of Christ rather than in some sense propitiating him. In any case, if propitiation has any right to a place in the Christian vocabulary, it belongs exclusively as a view of the atonement only insofar as it helps to express passion, feeling, power, rather than that Christ actually makes the Father forget his anger at us.[10] At the Table of Holy Communion we can only come as paupers, to make our plea, our suffrage, our prayer to the Father.

The tale of Eeyore's birthday in the Winnie-the-Pooh stories perhaps illustrates this best of all. The animals decide to give the poor old donkey, Eeyore, what they themselves would like. So Pooh bear gives him a jar of honey. Piglet gives him a balloon. Both honey and balloon are dearly loved by their respective donors but are of little potential use to the birthday boy. On the way to present the gifts, impatience takes over the donors. Pooh consumes all the honey, and Piglet blows up the balloon and then it bursts! The real secret of offering gifts at the Eucharist is that God is prepared to accept our own tired clapped-out fruits, not because they will do him any good, but because *we* need them.

NOTES

1. See text in Jasper/Cuming, op.cit., p.101 (later Byzantine text). We have translated the Greek word *prospherontes* as 'bringing', rather than 'offering'.
2. Paul Bradshaw, 'The Use and Abuse of Patristics', in Stevenson, ed., *Liturgy Reshaped*, p.143.
3. See Stevenson, *Eucharist and Offering* (New York, Pueblo, 1986), pp.20ff., and 34ff.
4. See Mark Santer's Foreword to *Eucharist and Offering*, pp.vii–viii.
5. See Colin Buchanan, *The End of the Offertory – An Anglican Study*, Grove Liturgical Study 14 (Bramcote, Grove, 1978), pp.19f.
6. *Lutheran Book of Worship* (Minneapolis, Augsburg Publishing House/Philadelphia, Board of Publication, Lutheran Church in America, 1978), p.109.
7. *The Book of Common Prayer* (New York, Seabury, 1979), p.369 (Eucharistic Prayer B, from Rite II).
8. See Max Thurian, 'The eucharistic memorial, sacrifice of praise and supplication', in M. Thurian, ed., *Ecumenical Perspectives on Baptism, Eucharist and Ministry*, Faith and Order Paper 116 (Geneva, World Council of Churches, 1983), p.102.
9. David N. Power, *The Sacrifice We Offer* (Edinburgh, T. & T. Clark, 1987).
10. See Kenneth Stevenson, 'Eucharistic Sacrifice – an insoluble liturgical problem?', forthcoming in *The Scottish Journal of Theology* 42 (1989).

6

OURSELVES, OUR SOULS AND BODIES

⚜

Were the whole realm of nature mine
That were an offering far too small.
Love so amazing, so divine,
Demands my soul, my life, my all

(Isaac Watts)[1]

1

Isaac Watts did not write these words, taken from the last verse of the well-known hymn, 'When I survey the wondrous cross', for Holy Week. He wrote them for the Eucharist. It is probably true to say that most people are familiar with it as a *seasonal* hymn, and they would only think of singing it at a Eucharist if it were celebrated during Passiontide. Such is the passage of time from the eighteenth-century Congregationalist tradition to our own that we take for granted the liturgical year. The cross so vigorously depicted in the stanzas of this rhetorically simple but profoundly moving hymn can, for us, only refer indirectly to the Christ of the Supper.

But the Eucharist is not just a cultic act, an indulgence by the Church. It is also a celebration of the reality of Christ. As we have seen so far, the way different people perceive the Christ event varies according to their tradition, culture, environment. And in an ecumenical age, in which travel is easy, people are able to identify with these traditions that much more easily. European holidays enable people of this country, otherwise isolated, to observe the reformed rites of Catholicism. Holy Land tours provide people with an opportunity to savour the liturgies of the East that have been the basis of so many of our reflections in these pages. But how is the connection between Supper and Lord ultimately made?

Underneath the differences of emphasis as well as the direct controversies, two discernible attitudes can be detected, even if they may often find expression in the same prayer. First, there is the liturgical psychology of the Church standing before God and doing something. This is the earliest form of the Eucharist, as found in the liturgy of Hippolytus, as well as the Byzantine prayers. This is why the Church *offers up* praise and prayer, and presents its gifts. Second, there is the liturgical psychology of *asking God to accept* what we are doing, whether it is just ourselves, or what we are praying, or what we are presenting. Many Reformation prayers stem from such an approach to God, although the Roman Canon combines both approaches, and there are many Eastern prayers that ask for acceptance as much as they present prayer and praise and gift.

Each approach is equally confident, although perhaps the edge can be given to the former, because it assumes that what the Church does *will* be accepted; it must be added that many a confident prayer needs to be counterbalanced by a good dose of penitence and preparation. Penitence and preparation are endemic to Christian prayer, as witness the way in which they appear in many guises, as we showed earlier on in this study.

But in what sense does Christ link us in the Supper? The New Testament affords us many models for Christology, but it is from the High Priestly image of the Epistle to the Hebrews that we find many liturgies feeling for ideas to express the union of earthly and heavenly. Although the anamnesis started life as a memorial of Christ's death and resurrection, it soon grew into an almost overflowing catalogue of Christ's ministry, moving forwards also to his ascension, his session at the Father's right hand, and his intercession there. But many Syrian prayers include an even fuller treatment, so that the Eucharist does not just com-memorate Christ from his death onwards, but moves back in time, to recount the main events of his life. The World

74

Council of Churches' 'Lima Liturgy' is a fine (if slightly verbose) example of this. Its anamnesis moves like this:

Wherefore Lord,
we celebrate today the memorial of our redemption:
we recall the birth and life of your Son among us,
his baptism by John, his last meal with the apostles,
his death and descent to the abode of the dead;
we proclaim Christ's resurrection and ascension in glory,
where as our Great High Priest he ever intercedes for all
    people;
and we look for his coming at the last.
United in Christ's priesthood, we present to you
this memorial: remember the sacrifice of your Son and
    grant to people everywhere the benefits
of Christ's redemptive work.[2]

There is certainly everything here. But even some of the Reformation Churches that have shown reserve in the very concept of a eucharistic prayer would find it hard to quarrel with the orthodoxy of this prayer. The difficulty is that when a prayer elaborates its theology, certain apologetic problems are raised. Two are critical.

First of all, the traditional Reformation insistence on Christ's saving work as single and complete runs the risk of nailing Christ so firmly to the cross as to render him immobile. We know this piety well, since it tends to see the Eucharist in Good Friday rather than Easter Day terms. If Christ has done it all, is there anything left that can be done, except surrender to his love? And yet there is, because the immobile Christ seems to need no response at all.

This brings us to the second problem – the relationship between the offering of the Christian and the offering of Christ. If the believer is able to offer self to God (Romans 12:1), then there must be some way in which this offering is rendered effective. Put in devotional terms, the individual Christian cannot be a Christian in isolation from Christ himself. So often art and music provide a helpful ambience for this dynamic relationship to be fed.

Yet again, the key is one of paradox. Christ's offering is single and complete, but it is of such significance that it transmutes itself – as well as those benefited by it – from history into eternity. Such is the message of the Watts hymn, couched as it is in the Pietism of its time, the individual hovering before the cross, as an eternal symbol of the reality of Christ's work for us. The need for images of this sort does not stem from a desire to maintain traditional pictures, but rather in order to continue to speak of the meaning and purpose of God as an everpresent reality among ordinary people today. Here the language of offering and of the movement from humanity to God and from God to humanity reaches its analogical limitations. Talk about the self-offering of Jesus to the Father corresponds only to the experience that Christians have of being accepted by God, being affirmed and forgiven by him. It is only logical and natural that this acceptance should find a focus in the Eucharist, as long as the Church does not become the earthly tail that wags the heavenly dog!

This brings us to some of the questions raised by liturgical formulations. Prayers that are lengthy and full, such as Lima, are bound to want to say everything several times over, as witness the overlap between the thanksgiving series in this rite and the anamnesis paragraph just quoted. On the other hand, prayers which are brief have to be equally carefully written so that what they say is precise, but sufficiently rhythmical to bear constant use. In an age that is replete with eucharistic prayers of every shape and size, we need to look for quality and variety; quality, in really fine phrases, variety in such a way that exposes people to different ways of saying the same thing, without subjecting them to gross liturgical instability. Playing around with the liturgy can become a bit of an indulgence, and those who do so should act with a sense of reverence, because they are tampering with the language whereby people ritualize their relationship with Christ.

Hymnody often manages to paint the picture more effectively than the language of liturgical prayer. Watts is one example. Wesley[3] produces language and symbolism richer still:

> For us he ever intercedes
> His heaven-deserving passion pleads,
> Presenting us before the throne;
> We want no sacrifice beside,
> By that great Offering sanctified,
> One with our Head, for ever One.

The union of earthly and heavenly is eloquently and aptly expressed thus:

> Our mean imperfect sacrifice
> On thine is as a burden thrown;
> Both in a common flame arise
> And both in God's account are one.

Here, the union echoes the communion of believers with one another, a theme also elaborated in the Wesley repertoire.

Modern hymns often use ancient models. Others, perhaps returning to more ancient traditions, depict Christ acting in the celebration itself. Brian Wren's[4] most ecstatic eucharistic hymn contemplates the footwashing (John 13), and has a verse as follows:

> Then take the towel, and break the bread,
> and humble us, and call us friends.
> Suffer and serve till all are fed,
> and show how grandly love intends
> to work till all creation sings
> to fill all worlds, to crown all things.

Here once more is a paradox, the Christ who stoops to exalt, and, more important still, the Christ who can place the *particular* congregation of one eucharistic celebration in the cosmic context of a restored creation.

2

The self-oblation of the believer can be a reality only if the believer has a person to offer, heart and soul. But what of the theme of self-oblation in Christianity? It is already there in Isaiah 6, with the temple vision, and we have noted it in Romans 12. It is strong in traditional spirituality, as witness *The Cloud of Unknowing*, which calls it the 'naked entent unto God', thus using a natural expression to show that self-offering does build on an instinct within the human person. But there are three important aspects of self-oblation which lie at the heart of the Eucharist.

The first we have already covered, namely intercession. In the prayer for Church and world, the community gathers together its concerns, both local and universal, and is challenged by what it can or cannot do, according to its self-perceptions, its self-image. This is, at the most practical level, a powerful image of the offering of self to God.

The second is the stage in the Eucharist when the Church formally offers itself to God and asks to be accepted. Although it is variously expressed in today's rites and hymnody, it naturally finds a focus when, in the eucharistic prayer, we ask for the blessing of the Spirit on our own corporate life. As one of the prayers in the Alternative Service Book puts it:

> Renew us by your Spirit,
> inspire us with your love,
> and unite us in the body of your Son.

Perhaps on the bland side, it is more than matched by a corresponding petition from the 1985 Canadian *Book of Alternative Services*:

> Send your Holy Spirit upon us
> and upon these gifts,
> that all who eat and drink at this table
> may be one body and one holy people,
> a living sacrifice in Jesus Christ, our Lord.[5]

This explicit language of sacrifice hits the nail on the head, and being 'one body and one holy people' is thus saved from appearing to be part of a cosy, holy huddle. Communion costs.

The third aspect is the much wider focus of the whole Eucharist as self-oblation, part of that reciprocal movement of God and humanity discussed earlier in this chapter. The importance of this feature may perhaps have decided Cranmer, after the experiment in 1549, to reposition the prayer of oblation *after* Communion. In this respect, Watts follows the same logic in the hymn with which we began:

> When I survey the wondrous cross . . .
> Forbid it, Lord, that I should boast . . .
> See from his head, his hands, his feet . . .

Only after contemplating these realities is the faithful prepared to offer himself, even though that is 'an offering far too small'.

It is a moot point whether self-oblation belongs before or after Communion. The matter is less controversial than it once was. Protestants have been conscious of the need to place it in the later position (along with Cranmer), in order to make the point that it is only after sharing Communion that we are ready to offer ourselves to God. But this sort of controversy is not really of great significance. When are we ready, in any case? Surely the moment of self-oblation cannot be a 'magic moment'. It is too much a part of Christian spirituality to belong exclusively in any one position. A modern text which has some of the traditional ring about it tries to capture some of the nuances we have been aware of in this discussion:

> Father, as we plead his sacrifice made once for all on the
> cross,
> we recall his dying and rising in glory,
> and we rejoice that he prays for us at your right hand.
> Pour out your Holy Spirit over us and these gifts
> which we bring before you from your own creation;
> show them to be for us the Body and Blood of your dear
> Son.

Make us one Body in Christ, a living sacrifice,
to serve you acceptably as a royal priesthood.[6]

The dialectic of human action and Christ event is kept intact throughout this paragraph, and the notion of 'pleading' makes the Eucharist a reality, but one that avoids the two traditional Western pitfalls, Catholic mechanism, and Protestant memorialism. Caricatures though they may well appear, they are nonetheless almost heresies, because, being logical and tidy, they avoid the rich ambiguity that should be inherent to the life of the Eucharist.

3

Whether self-oblation is explicitly prayed in the eucharistic prayer, or whether it comes in the prayer after Communion, this brings us fittingly to how the Eucharist should end. When the congregation prays (as it frequently does), 'Through him we offer you our souls and bodies, to be a living sacrifice. Send us out in the power of your Spirit, to live and work to your praise and glory', it is often in anticipation of the coffee-hour that these words are uttered. Sometimes it would be a sobering experience if those going so cheerfully from our warm and comfortable fellowships were to feel and breathe the air of hostility and persecution faced by so many other Christians in many parts of the world.

How the Eucharist should end has not been a greatly debated subject, largely because it has been taken for granted. Cranmer clearly wanted to give his rite some substance, so that the Gloria in excelsis was shifted from the opening section of the service, where it had been in the Middle Ages and where he had placed it in 1549. To reposition it at the end made the Communion end on a note of praise and thanksgiving, together with a petition for healing and forgiveness. And still here, in the Gloria, there is the theme of the unexpected and the contradictory, for the image of Jesus as the Lamb depicts the one who has been slain, and yet lives for ever, to be worshipped, adored, and served. ·

In the modern rites, the ending of the Eucharist tends to be weak, to the point of being functional. True, the Roman Mass before 1970 was full of accretions, such as the Last Gospel, and was cluttered with devotional prayers. Perhaps Cranmer's incomparable liturgy of Communion did take too long to end. But we are now left with a stark, clinical conclusion:

- silence (in many rites)
- post-Communion prayer (sometimes two, and in Anglican and Methodist rites said by all)
- blessing
- dismissal

The liturgical pundits of the 1960s were very enthusiastic about that spirituality which carries the banner, 'after the vision – the task'. It could be that a balance is now needed and that liturgies, whether sung or said, need to end more gradually. Silence is not part of the liturgical tradition of many of those Churches that use a formal service-book. Silence is a way of getting distractions identified, and of drinking in the goodness and providence of God. Many rites recommend it after the lections. It could certainly be appropriate after the homily. Many congregations use it fruitfully during, or at the end of, the intercession. But after Communion, silence is often squeezed out, in the rush to get the liturgy over.

This is not a happy state of affairs, and clergy frequently act with insensitivity to those many people who come to church, after a week of high stress and too much activity. As someone once remarked, 'We come for spiritual refreshment, to get a break from the lives we lead the rest of the time.' But if people are going to have silence, they need to learn to use it better. It has sometimes been said that forty-five seconds is a good starter, because it is long enough to get into, not too long to become embarrassing for those who are by nature restless. (I do not, by the way, subscribe to the view that children are incapable of sitting still in a liturgy. It is often the adults that cannot cope with it!) They also need some help, too, with how to start the silence in their own minds. Maybe they will have something that they want to think about, from one of the hymns, or from the sermon. Perhaps there is a short passage of Scripture that comes to mind. And there is a further dimension: the silence is corporate. Congregations often build up their own sense of corporate identity by sitting in a prolonged silence. Talkative modern Christianity can learn a few lessons in depth.

Post-Communion prayers vary from one tradition to another. Many of the Roman Catholic prayers (which are variable, with the collect, and the prayer over the gifts at the offertory) are too short to make a solid impact. The long prayer in the Alternative Service Book, on the other hand, is a popular compilation, perhaps because it paints a picture that people can relate to readily:

> Father of all, we give you thanks and praise
> that when we were still far off
> you met us in your Son and brought us home . . .

The Canadian *Book of Alternative Services* (1985) makes provision for a variable post-Communion (often modelled on the Roman), which is followed by a bold doxology, recited by the congregation:

> Glory to God,
> whose power, working in us,
> can do infinitely more
> than we ask or imagine.
> Glory to God from generation to generation,
> in the Church and in Christ Jesus,
> for ever and ever. [7]

Such a collective note may well serve to draw the service to the right kind of thankful conclusion.

The popular reaction to the new concluding rites, however, has been mixed. It is perhaps a measure of the need to end more smoothly, less angularly, that this part of the liturgy needs a fresh look, particularly in the transition from blessing to dismissal, when many people want to have a time of quiet. This would be dealt with if the proper position for the silence, immediately after Communion, were observed. But the dismissal, like the Peace, is easily trivialized. It is not an announcement – but a command.

The key to the concluding part of the Eucharist is that it is supposed to bring home to the gathered community its own oblation of itself. Responsibilities lie outside, and for some people they will be ever-pressing. It could be that the service has, somehow, provided an important answer to a difficult problem. For much of the time, the Eucharist just helps people to carry their burdens, making them no more than bearable. But the psychology of the conclusion is to help the people of God come down from the mountain to the plain, in joyful thanksgiving. That makes the choice of hymnody, crucial elsewhere, important here too.

Perhaps overdoing how to end a service, the Danish Lutheran rite ends in a way that balances the start. After Communion, there is a short thanksgiving prayer by the pastor, followed by the blessing. During the hymn which follows, the pastor removes the outer liturgical garments, and reappears at the altar for the concluding prayer, said by a layperson, which gives thanks for the time of worship. In many places the congregation remains seated for the organ voluntary, which comes only at this point. Good liturgical music can help the liturgy regain some subtlety. Many Eucharists are enlivened by good organ music, whether reflective (during Communion) or more abrasive (as Postludium). The baldness of recent revisions could be compensated for by imaginative singing or instrumental music.

Watts' hymn may be too vivid a picture, too literal in its overall motifs. Such is the representational piety of the tradition he stood in. But there are times when pictures are necessary. Just as there are varied ways of portraying the notion of offering in the Eucharist, so there are different ways of depicting the work of Christ. Pictures, and more so, icons, have a habit of drawing the beholder into their midst, especially by such devices as inverted perspectives, and imaginative use of colour. Of course, tastes will vary. But many hymns in the Western tradition, I suspect, provide the same foundation for piety as iconography does for the Eastern Churches. Each is a celebration of the wonders of God. Each has an eye for the past as well as for the present and the future. Each medium is built on a series of disciplines that makes it what it is. It is true to say that many modern Christians who want to take the new rites to their hearts, and who are even prepared to see them improved in the next round of revisions, have used, and will continue to use, hymnody as a cushion on which to rest themselves, so that their piety is inched forward at a more convenient rate. It is not just Methodism that was born in song.

NOTES

1. See notes in Maurice Frost, ed., *Historical Companion to Hymns Ancient and Modern* (London, Clowes, 1962), p.196. It is interesting that the original text has 'a *present* far too small'.
2. See text in Thurian, ed., *Ecumenical Perspectives on Baptism, Eucharist and Ministry*, Faith and Order Paper 116 (Geneva, World Council of Churches, 1983), p.243.
3. See text in J. Ernest Rattenbury, *The Eucharistic Hymns of John and Charles Wesley* (London, Epworth, 1948), p.232 (no.117, stanza 2), and p.242 (no.147, stanza 4).
4. *Hymns Ancient and Modern New Standard* (1983), no.489, stanza 4.
5. *The Book of Alternative Services of the Anglican Church of Canada* (Toronto, Anglican Book Centre, 1985), p.195 (Eucharistic Prayer 1).
6. Text drafted for the Church of England Liturgical Commission.
7. *The Book of Alternative Services*, p.214.

7

AN OFFERING
FAR TOO SMALL . . .

✤

Jesus, Lord and Master,
who served your disciples in washing their feet;
serve us often, serve us daily,
in washing our motives, our ambitions, our actions;
that we may share with you in your mission to the world
and serve others gladly for your sake;
to whom be glory for ever.   (David Silk)[1]

1

Prayers addressed to Christ have gone out of fashion, but
they often make fine devotions, because they have about
them an intensity of feeling frequently lacking in the formal
prayers addressed to the Father. David Silk's prayer was
inspired by a passage from the writings of Michael Ramsey.
It serves to show that the repertoire of eucharistic piety has
not been exhausted by two thousand years of history.
Indeed it has not. Two millennia of variety, schism,
controversy – and great richness – have managed to provoke
from millions of Christian women and men the response to
Christ that his Supper is worth celebrating, whatever the
circumstances. What does this book hope to add? It does not
seek to be a finely balanced systematic theology. Nor has it
attempted to say everything. But it *does* say that certain
features of the Eucharist are in danger of neglect, and that
there are certain parts of the common tradition that can help
us out of the conundrum.

First of all, the language of offering, like that of
memorial, is rich and varied. No one branch of Christianity
'owns' sacrifice, least of all that branch which has been most

vocal about it. It is rather the eternal offering of Christ which owns *us*.

Second, the notion of offering, for all that it is a metaphor, is still a supremely appropriate way of helping Christians relate to their lives, not just to worship at Church services. As so much modern literature shows (the popular press included), people can still think of sacrifice and grasp the meaning.

Third, the truth of offering is one of paradox and ambiguity. It is paradoxical because it holds together seemingly contradictory opposites, that Christ prays for us (as the image goes) at the Father's hand, but still stoops to be with us as we gather round the table. It is ambiguous because the bread and wine of the meal are at one and the same time the stuff of sustenance, but are also signs of the creation that will one day be restored in all things. To sit down to eat and drink together is itself a sign of sacrifice, because it seals a binding commitment between and among those who dare to do so.

Fourth, the attitude of offering means that it is a serious activity of the Church. Commitment is not mere words, but costs and hurts. Too many Christian congregations drop in for a Eucharist in much the same way as someone drops in for a drink. Perhaps this means that the Church should take far greater stock of non-eucharistic worship, for *all* worship is sacrificial.

2

What might this mean? It means seeing the present liturgies in provisional terms, as were their predecessors. It means being able to see them as tools of the trade of working for the Kingdom of God. It means approaching them with a sense of awe and reverence, for all that they may appear in paperback form, because they point us all to a life of selfgiving and sacrifice. In these pages, we have tried to alert Christians to the possibility of seeing the sacrificial aspect of the Eucharist in much wider terms than most Westerners have been in the habit of doing for centuries. But by now it will have become clear that such an orientation is not so unusual, given the rich tradition that has fed us on this journey. It involves intricate questions that have not been fully solved by separated Christians. It also involves liturgies that are, at times, rather lapidary and self-conscious in the way they handle sacrifice. But the fact that the issue is problematical perhaps stems from the very neglect of this theme in eucharistic spirituality. How could it be summarized?

I suggest, in conclusion, that there are three inherent movements of sacrifice in the Eucharist, which belong together, yet are distinct. The first is that of *story*. We recount the story of salvation in reading the Word and preaching about it. And we recount it in a different and more formal manner when the eucharistic prayer is recited and when the praise of God is sung in sacred song. The story is our sacrifice of praise, because it is the story of the renewal of our commitment to God.

The second is that of *response*. We listen to the story, but we also act upon it, hearing and receiving the Word, and praying for the needs of the world. We involve ourselves in the mighty acts of God by placing the Eucharist in the context of that history of salvation that will go on until the end of time. The Church is not just a passive recipient of what God does. The Church is servant of Christ and therefore dares to act boldly in imitation of him. To dare to stand before God and 'do' the Eucharist is part of that response.

The third is that of *gift*. Here we come to the most sensitive part of all, not just because of the controversies of the past, but because of the paradox that in bread and wine God speaks to us, in ordinary food that is itself the result of dying and rising, corn crushed and baked, grapes crushed and fermented. In acted parable, as of old, Jesus plays it slant. The bread and wine are neither formally 'offered' nor ritually 'held back'. They are just there, on the table, eloquent testimony of the final meal that we hope to share at the end of time.

NOTE

1. David Silk, *Prayers for use at the Alternative Services* (London, Mowbrays, 1986^2), p.86 (no.248).